A day in the life

A day in the life

in the

life

A glimpse into the **CHAOS**—AND **HOPE**—
of families with children living in the grip of
chronic mental health disorders

BEV ROOZEBOOM

PUBLISHING + DESIGN

Print ISBN: 978-1-7323526-0-5
E-Book ISBN: 978-1-7323526-5-0

Published and printed in the United States of America by the Write Place, Inc. For more information, please contact:

the Write Place, Inc.
809 W. 8th Street, Suite 2
Pella, Iowa 50219
www.thewriteplace.biz

Cover and interior design by Michelle Stam, the Write Place, Inc. Cover stock photo by irina88w, thinkstock.com.

Copies of this book may be ordered online at Amazon and BarnesandNoble.com.

View other Write Place titles at www.thewriteplace.biz.

DEDICATION

To Steve: What a gift to be able to share the journey together. God truly made us partners in every way. You are loved beyond words.

In loving memory of my mom, Revena Gritters (03/26/34–04/04/18). My heart aches with longing to give you one more hug, to share one more cup of tea. I rest in the joy of knowing that your deep, humble love for Jesus and others lives on. What a blessing to be connected to your legacy of faith.

CONTENTS

INTRODUCTION

I often wish I had a degree in psychology! It would have been very helpful for me as a mom. A quick glance at the stack of books in our bookcase sheds light on what life has looked like in our home for the past two-plus decades. Books with titles such as *Dare to Discipline[1]*, *The Strong-Willed Child[2]* and *Bringing Up Boys[3]* were my starting-out books as we tried to understand—and deal with—our young son's behaviors. I soon discovered, however, that we were on a different playing field altogether. As we went through our son's growing-up years, books such as *The Explosive Child[4]* and *The Bipolar Child[5]* graced my nightstand. Now, early into our son's adult years, you will find well-marked copies of books such as *Why Do Christians Shoot Their Wounded?[6]*, *Ministry With Persons With Mental Illness and Their Families[7]*, *Troubled Minds: Mental Illness and the Church's Mission[8]* and *Surviving Schizophrenia: A Family Manual.[9]*

It turns out the familiar childhood taunt, "It takes one to know one," really is correct! I am a mom of a much-loved son who has struggled with mental health issues all his life. No, I don't have a degree in psychology, but I do have an intimate view—a mom's view—of severe mental illness and how it affects the entire family. I have never counseled clients as a behavioral therapist, or diagnosed young children as a psychologist, or prescribed medicine as a psychiatrist, but I do have the lived experience of a mom in the trenches. I am fully aware of the chaos mental illness brings to a home. I understand the heartache of not being able to soothe away the emotional pain a child feels. I've experienced the grief that comes with knowing our love is simply not enough to heal. I comprehend the frustration of navigating the maze of a broken mental health care system, and I've lived through the nightmare of dealing with the criminal justice system. I know firsthand the pain of being misunderstood and unfairly judged by others. I've also experienced deep bouts of self-condemnation and a sense of failure when things are going poorly in the home. I'm well-acquainted with the embarrassment, the isolation and the stigma that accompanies a child who marches to a completely different beat—on a whole other playing field.

Yet in the midst of the turmoil and frequent roller coaster emotions, God has given me a precious gift. HOPE. Deep, abiding hope.

The above-mentioned books were and are great in helping me better understand the psychological make-up of my son and how to best manage difficult situations, especially through the lens of a Christian world and life view. Yet I've come to realize that simply understanding the psychology behind brain disorders is not the same as experiencing *hope*. I've discovered only one place where I've been able to find that reassuring sense of peace and confident expectation that, ultimately, things *will* be okay—and that is in the arms of Jesus.

As we spend time with Jesus, we begin to discover His view of life is different than ours. We sense His gaze is often focused on things we can't yet see or understand. We recognize His perspective is much wider and broader than ours. When we look around us and see only the darkness of mental illness, Jesus invites us to look through His lens—through His eyes. As we do, we're surprised to discover that Jesus has tucked away a cache of secret riches and hidden treasures in the most unlikely places.

The beautiful promise in Scripture that led to the birth of this book lies in Isaiah 45:3:

I will give you treasures hidden in the darkness — secret riches.
I will do this so you may know that I am the Lord, the God of
Israel, the one who calls you by name (NLT).

Every parent of a child struggling with a mental illness or an emotional disorder will occasionally find themselves in extremely dark and stressful circumstances. There will be seasons when their child's illness flares up and instability threatens to topple the entire household; times when their marriage creaks and strains under the weight of parenting such a difficult child; dark days when God seems distant, cold and uncaring; situations that leave them breathlessly wondering what good could possibly come out of such anguish.

Indeed, life often seems overwhelming when walking alongside someone in the grip of mental illness. We may find it hard to believe there are treasures to be found and riches to be mined in the darkness of such a deep pit. When we find ourselves stumbling about in the gloom — anxious, fearful and alone — Jesus delights in illuminating the darkness to show us He was always there. When we look around and see only death and ashes, He invites us to look deeper — to see the potential for great beauty and abundant life. When we despair over how weak, tired and helpless we are, Jesus is thrilled to be our strength and enable us to reach heights we thought impossible.

No one is exempt from dark, dangerous and difficult circumstances. We will all suffer in this world. But those who have a living, vibrant relationship with Jesus Christ will not be left to wander the long path alone. We have One who promises to walk each step of the way with us. His light will surround us, and not even the darkness of mental illness can overwhelm it. In this we find our hope, even in the midst of chaos.

The thought of my suffering…
is bitter beyond words.
I will never forget this awful time,
as I grieve over my loss.
Yet I still dare to hope
when I remember this:

"The faithful love of the Lord never ends!
His mercies never cease.
Great is his faithfulness;
his mercies begin afresh each morning.
I say to myself, The Lord is my inheritance;
therefore, I will hope in him!" (Lam. 3:19-24, NLT).

My prayer for each of us on this adventure through life is that the God of all hope will fill us with joy and peace as we trust in Him. May we be blessed to know and experience the overwhelming love of Jesus as we journey with Him.

Bev Roozeboom

PREFACE

I am a collector of quotes, and you will find many of them sprinkled throughout this book. One of my favorites is an excerpt from Timothy Keller's encouraging book, *Walking With God Through Pain and Suffering*. Ponder these powerful words:

> …Very often God does not give us exactly what we ask for. Instead He gives us what we would have asked for if we had known everything He knows.[1]

He gives us what we would have asked for if we had known everything He knows. As our lives unfold day by day, year by year, we can often look back over the span of time and connect the dots, gaining some semblance of understanding the *whys* of certain events. But in many other instances, God holds His cards close to His chest and never fully reveals what He alone knows, mysteries we are not privy to. God knows faith grows strongest in the dark. When life is an enigma, God asks us to simply trust Him, to believe He is good—even when the script of our life seems to be written with a foreign pen.

How well I understand that. I wonder how many times I've looked back over the circumstances and events of my life and the lives of those I love and thought, *It wasn't supposed to be like this. This wasn't the script I would have written.*

The Backstory

In the spring of 1993, my husband, Steve, and I were blessed to adopt our son Kyle, a darling two-month-old baby boy. This precious little boy had huge brown eyes and tons of spunk and energy! We were filled with love—and endless dreams—for our son. As days progressed into weeks, weeks into months and months into years, we began to realize that the "spunk and energy" that characterized our son were actually outward signs of something much more significant. As time went on, it became clearly evident that Kyle's intense drive was not the normal energetic activity of a toddler or school-aged child. As his behaviors became increasingly more challenging, we sought out doctors and therapists who could help us make sense of what we were dealing with. Along the way, Kyle was diagnosed with a variety of mental health disorders. In second grade, he was diagnosed with ADHD. In fourth grade, a psychologist added generalized anxiety disorder and oppositional defiant disorder to his earlier diagnosis. In Kyle's middle school years, his psychiatrist began treating him for early-onset bipolar disorder; finally, in his early twenties, Kyle was diagnosed with schizophrenia.

You will find parts of our life story sprinkled throughout the pages of this book. The title, *A Day in the Life,* was a term Steve and I frequently used to describe some of the crazy-making days we so often experienced in our family. Roller coaster rides of soaring highs followed by plunging lows were our daily norm. We would often "make sense" of our angst and frustration by reminding ourselves— somewhat tongue in cheek—"it's just another day in the life!"

But this book is not just about us. *A Day in the Life* was written primarily for and about families who have a son or daughter living with a chronic mental illness, personality disorder or a brain disorder* of any kind. Families whose children struggle with these issues day in and day out often experience a completely different kind of "normal"—one that is often fraught with chaos, confusion and exhaustion.

In preparation for this book, I had the privilege of interviewing several parents with children ranging in age from seven to those in their forties and fifties. The parents interviewed have children with a wide variety of diagnoses spanning the alphabet: antisocial personality disorder, anxiety disorders, attention deficit disorder, autism spectrum disorder, bipolar disorder, borderline personality disorder, depression, dissociative identity disorder, disruptive mood dysregulation disorder, fetal alcohol syndrome, oppositional defiance disorder, pervasive developmental disorder, posttraumatic stress disorder, reactive attachment disorder, schizophrenia, sensory processing disorder and traumatic brain injury.† I was touched and amazed by the faith, resilience, dedication and unconditional love of these moms and dads. They openly shared their stories and their hearts, even as some deeply personal questions were asked.‡

Each chapter of *A Day in the Life* examines a different theme and is divided into three parts. The first section, **A Glimpse Inside**, is designed to open the eyes and hearts of those who misunderstand mental illness, as well as lower the walls of isolation many disheartened families live behind. Parents and family members, as well as the "outside world," will be invited to witness a day in the life of several families who have children with a mental health disorder.

---

* *Throughout this book, the terms "mental health disorder," "mental illness," "emotional illness," "emotional disorder," "personality disorder," "mood disorder" and "brain disorder" are used interchangeably to describe the various mental and emotional difficulties addressed.*

† *These and other mental health disorders are defined in the Glossary, located in the back of the book.*

‡ *Names and minor details have been changed to protect the individuals and their families. In many instances, the person or story described is actually a composite of several people or many individual stories.*

Because of the pervasive stigma of mental illness, many parents suffer in silence, believing no one could possibly understand their struggles. They do not freely share with their friends, churches or even their own families the never-ending challenges and fears they live with on a daily basis. As common threads of mental illness are revealed, parents will recognize elements of their own stories and be assured they are not the only ones walking this difficult path.

The overriding purpose of *A Day in the Life*, however, is to offer Living Water to discouraged parents. This purpose is most clearly articulated in the second section of each chapter, **Gazing Up**. The theme verse for this book, found in Isaiah 45:3, offers an intriguing promise: *"I will give you treasures hidden in the darkness – secret riches. I will do this so you may know that I am the Lord…the one who calls you by name" (NLT).* As layers of darkness and confusion are peeled away, hidden gems of God's heart are brought to light. The readers will uncover inspiring truth that comforts aching souls and replenishes weary emotions. Parents will be assured of God's equipping and be given the courage to keep pressing forward. Additional Scripture passages applicable to the chapter's topic, as well as a personal prayer, are also included in this section.

The third and final part of each chapter invites readers to look deeper into their own hearts. **Going Deeper – Getting Personal** includes three questions designed to be used in personal study or in a group setting.

Yes, *A Day in the Life* is the story of courageous parents everywhere who deeply love a child living in the grip of mental illness. But ultimately, it is the story of a loving Redeemer who steps into the swirling chaos and invites His children to discover a treasure trove of hope – even in the darkness.

CHAPTER ONE

A Day in the Life: Chaos in the Home

A GLIMPSE INSIDE

Recently I received a wonderfully refreshing email from a new neighbor. She and her husband have several young children, and their youngest son has autism. Apparently he loves the outdoors and will occasionally "escape," ending up in a neighbor's yard or deck. They wanted the neighborhood to be aware of who their child is and to contact them immediately if we saw their child outside unattended. I appreciated this honest email, as it gave us a glimpse into their home life, making us somewhat aware of their reality. *Somewhat.*

I have a hunch, though, that this was only a *glimpse,* a small peek into what this family lives with 24/7. My neighbor's email spoke of plans to get special locks and alarms for their windows and doors, as well as a medical ID for their child. It's no small job being vigilant and attentive day in and day out, especially with several other children in their home to love and care for. There must be a high level of exhaustion and weariness that depletes them daily. I'm sure they often experience chaos in their home.

Chaos in the home is too often the reality of our families, especially if we have a child in our home struggling with a mental health disorder. A day in the life of many of our families would never make the cut for a Hallmark movie.

How well I remember those early years. Our son does not have autism, but his growing-up years were marked with chaotic activity. I recently came across a journal from when Kyle was around ten years old. It reminded me of a typical "day in the life" with our son:

> Another hard morning. I was up half the night with Kyle, trying to get him back to sleep. When will he ever sleep through the night? Steve and I are exhausted, and this morning was awful. I was cranky and irritable; cross with the kids. Kyle, as usual, was intent on annoying his sister and terrorizing our poor dog. He fought me over what to wear (WHY are these changes of seasons so hard???), he adamantly refused to eat breakfast and he relentlessly demanded he be allowed to walk to school an hour early (I refused, but it sure was tempting).
>
> I was sapped by the time the kids left. As usual, I had a good cry on the way to work. Sometimes I almost wish I had a long commute—it's about the only time I have a little peace and quiet. This morning was especially rough, and I feel like a failure as a mom. Why was I so crabby? What a horrible way to send the kids into their day. Then, to add salt to the wound, I decided to stop for a donut at the convenience store. On the counter was a koozie that said, "THIS ISN'T THE

LIFE I SIGNED UP FOR!" I know it was supposed to be funny, but today, that's exactly how I feel. Oh Lord, I'm so sorry! What is wrong with me? Help me accept and enjoy this life You've given me. I do love my children—each and every one. Help me love them well.

As I look back on those early years, I remember the guilt, the self-condemnation, the grief and the ever-present weariness. Driving most of those emotions was the relentless *chaos*. Families who have a child with a severe emotional disorder predominantly describe living in turmoil and disarray. Oftentimes our children are able to hold it together while at school, but then let loose as soon as they get home. Frequently the outside world does not see what it's really like in our homes. They don't fully understand the daily challenges of living in such upheaval, never knowing what will set off the next explosion.

I remember having lunch several years ago with a group of moms whose children were reaching the end of their high school years. One mom lamented the passing of her son's youth, wishing they were back in those early, innocent years. All the other moms agreed with her sentiment, and I suppose I, too, made some vague comment in agreement, lacking the courage to be honest. But in my heart I was screaming, "No! I would *never* want to go back to those early years!"

When asked how they would describe the growing-up years with their child, many of the parents interviewed talked about the sheer chaos of those early years. The adjectives given were descriptive of the bedlam and pandemonium often found in their homes. Those years were depicted as stressful, remarkably difficult, beyond hard, extremely traumatic, volatile, scary, frustrating and bewildering. Parents talked of experiencing daily battles and daily strife; having to constantly be on their guard—locking doors and windows, as well as locking away scissors, knives and medicine; walking on eggshells; being hyper-vigilant—always waiting for the next explosion.

How well Liz and Jason understand this life-altering upheaval. This young couple, after years of struggling with infertility and the challenges of the adoption process, was thrilled when they were finally able to welcome their daughter, Beth, into her new forever home. Beth was adopted as a toddler from an Eastern Bloc country. Jason and Liz fully expected the transition time to be stressful, but they were pleasantly surprised that initially things were quite calm in their home. They realized their daughter acted younger than her peers and had some unique quirks, but they knew this was not unusual for a child adopted from another country. By age seven, however, their family life was no longer calm or peaceful. Beth had begun displaying some pretty significant behavioral issues, pointing to early signs of mental illness. Liz was quite certain something more than cultural differences or immaturity was going on. She said, "A parent just knows. The experts don't always catch it." Over time, Beth was diagnosed with autism spectrum disorder, fetal alcohol syndrome and, later, paranoid schizophrenia.

As Beth progressed into her pre-teen and teenage years, Jason and Liz's home life was marked by disarray and drama. Beth wanted friends, but she had no idea how to relate to her peers. She began to self-injure, frequently cutting herself. From time to time she would run away. She got into trouble at school. She lied more than she told the truth. She frequently lashed out against her parents.

Liz and Jason's world was rocked when Beth, in a fit of anger, called the police and told them her dad was physically abusing her. That accusation ushered their family into one of the darkest seasons of their life. The stigma followed Jason for months. Liz said they not only struggled with having Jason's reputation unjustly marred, they also feared having their younger daughter removed from the home because of Beth's accusations. Jason and Liz acknowledge it took a long time for their family relationships to regain a semblance of normalcy, and even now scars remain.

Liz and Jason's story is, unfortunately, not unique. Parents who have children with mood disorders and mental illnesses state unequivocally that all too often chaos reigns in their home. A simple parental "no" could set off a rage that lasts for hours. A change in their schedule could cause the day to erupt in upheaval. The wrong pair of socks or a scratchy shirt or a piece of toast unknowingly cut the "wrong way" are all potential minefields.

Kimberly can relate. Her daughter, Skylar, has a diagnosis of RAD—reactive attachment disorder. Kimberly shared, "Life with Skylar was extremely challenging, marked by daily battles. There was always another fire to put out. It was difficult to get even minimal cooperation, and I got so weary of the constant battle for control. It's sad to admit, but I have almost no good memories of Skylar's childhood years. Unfortunately, her adult years are off to a rocky start as well."

Chaos into adulthood

The discord of chaos often follows families as their children enter adulthood, even if the child is no longer living in their home. Most parents who have a son or daughter living with severe, chronic mental illness have discovered this journey to be a marathon, not a sprint. Mental illness and all its issues does not end at age eighteen—not for the child, nor for the parents. The challenges many of our children face as they strive to live and function in the adult world often bring confusion and a whole new set of difficulties.

When asked about what causes the most chaos in their lives now, the parents of adult children who were interviewed openly shared their ongoing frustrations.

Linda struggles with the drama her young adult daughter, Anne, creates around her—especially over social media. "Anne has no filters in place and puts extremely inappropriate stuff online for everyone to read. I cringe when I hear the latest from her friends. I don't understand why she does that. It's embarrassing and frustrating. Anne has always been, and continues to be, very moody. I never know from day to day how she'll respond or react to situations. We walk on eggshells around her."

More than one parent commented on the squalor their children choose to live in. "Alan's apartment is a pigsty," lamented Suzette. "It's grossly dirty to the point of being a health hazard. We've tried to help him keep it somewhat cleaned up, but he refuses to do anything for himself, even though he's capable. It's to the point we've decided to let it be. I'm making the choice to simply not go over there anymore."

Many parents, no matter what state they live in, expressed their frustration with the mental health system. Sharon said, "For me, the chaos comes when dealing with the mental health system. There is a constantly changing parade of people who are supposed to be helping Leah. It's so frustrating. Leah just gets used to one mental health provider and the game changes. It seems like we're constantly having to make adjustments. Recently Leah's psychiatrist retired, and the search for a replacement has been difficult. We live in a small state, and good psychiatrists are few and far between. We have so many other things demanding our time and energy, and I find it to be very draining to have to search so hard for adequate mental health care for our daughter. Then there's the paperwork.

Talk about chaos! It's very cumbersome and time-consuming, and it all falls on me."

Russ and Leslie shared that their recent turmoil comes from the constant fight to get Jillian the treatment she so desperately needs. "It's been a huge struggle," said Russ, "to get help for our daughter. We are constantly having to advocate for better care, proper treatment and so forth. To compound the problem, much of the time Jillian refuses to take her meds. She's unable to connect the dots of what *she* needs to do, so we find ourselves not only battling the mental health system but battling our daughter as well. Chaotic? Absolutely."

Ray and Trina say their consternation comes from trying to sort out their son's finances. "Our son Josh, now in his thirties, is a terrible money manager. His track record for holding down jobs is pretty spotty, so he never has much money. When a little money does come in, he either spends it immediately or someone finagles it away from him. He is constantly coming to us—wanting us to fix his finances, pay his bills or help him out of the latest mess. We struggle to differentiate between what's enabling him and what is actually helping him. It's a constant source of frustration for us."

For other parents, the chaos they feel stems from worrying about their adult children. Meredith confided, "I have such an ongoing concern for Chance's future. It's as if there's always a cloud on the horizon. I wonder if he'll be able to keep his job, stay out of trouble, experience meaningful relationships and so on."

Carolyn said much the same thing. "My daughter, Wendy, is always on my mind. Two years ago she walked away from us and now has nothing to do with us. I often find myself wondering where she is, what's she doing, if she's okay, etc. Even though the external, day-to-day chaos we used to deal with is gone, my 'chaos' now comes from the constant wondering, waiting."

Sheer chaos. Daily battles. Overwhelming difficulties. When our world is darkened by the swirling chaos of mental illness and emotional challenges, how do we function? Is there hope for our families?

GAZING UP

Is it possible to find peace in the chaos?

Many hurting parents said it was precisely in this very darkness where they finally learned what it meant to trust and rely on the Lord. Their search for true and lasting peace, in the midst of overwhelming chaos, brought them to the heart of Jesus.

Marcy admits there still are times she struggles with feeling resentful about the constant turmoil brought on by their son, Jacob. "I'm so often exhausted, fearful for our other kids, fearful for *Jacob*. But because of Jacob's severe emotional challenges, my husband, Travis, and I have learned what it really means to trust God. Jacob's issues have prompted Travis and me to pray together more often. I've spent a lot of time searching and studying Scripture. I've seen and experienced how the Holy Spirit has given me wisdom and specific words in various situations with Jacob, as well as with our other kids. The Spirit helps me through each day. He is truly my encourager."

Colleen said that even though their daughter, Maya, is no longer in their home, she's aware that a new crisis is always just a phone call away. Colleen shared, though, that her relationship with God has grown much deeper and more intimate because of all they've gone through with Maya. "I find myself listening to Him and talking with Him often. I'm learning to *intentionally* allow Him to be in control. I don't sleep a lot at night, so I use those quiet hours as my 'God time.'

He is always faithful to give me what I need for each new day. He always seems to give me the right thing at just the right time."

God is always faithful, even in the midst of turmoil. God gave me a beautiful image when our family was going through a very stormy season. We had recently experienced the traumatic death of my dad, and Kyle, who had been close to his grandpa, was struggling with extreme instability. One day, as I was quietly meditating on Scripture and spending time in prayer, God gave me a picture in my mind, reminding me He is always at work, even in the storms of life.

> In my mind's eye, I saw a tree, bent over and battered in a storm. The wind was raging and the rain lashing down. I came to realize I was that tree and the storm was a symbol of the tumultuous chaos our family was currently living in. But I was aware that even though the tree was being pummeled and was on the verge of toppling over, it was still standing. The trunk was not broken and the roots were secure, anchoring the tree solidly in place.

> Jesus reminded me this storm was serving to make my roots grow stronger...deeper. Then He whispered that He would not allow this stormy season to destroy me. He reassured me that when the time was right, He would say to the storm, "Peace! Be still!"

When our outer world is being rocked and we are spinning in the chaos, it's important to quiet our inner world. Jesus longs for us to sit in His presence and allow Him to calm us. He is here, even in the raging turmoil. He might not immediately calm the storm of our circumstances, but He will gently speak peace to our hearts. As a beautiful praise song expressed so well, "Sometimes He calms the storm, and other times He calms His child."[1] Invite Jesus into your chaos and allow Him to calm you. He is not panicked or intimidated by the raging storm.

"Be still and know that I am God" (Psalm 46:10, NIV).

Additional Scripture to meditate on

Remember who created you...?
    Who shaped you...?
  See, you have nothing to fear. I, who made you, will take you back.
    I have chosen you, named you as My own.
  When you face stormy seas I will be there with you with
        endurance and calm; you will not be engulfed in raging rivers.
  If it seems like you're walking through fire with flames licking
        at your limbs, keep going; you won't be burned.
  Because I, the Eternal One, am your God.
    I am the Holy One of Israel, and I will save you.
    You are special to Me and I love you. (Isaiah 43:1-4a, VOICE)

Now may the Lord of peace Himself grant you His peace at all times and in every way [that peace and spiritual well-being that comes to those who walk with Him, regardless of life's circumstances]. The Lord be with you all. (2 Thess. 3:16, AMP)

Do not be anxious about anything, but in every situation, by prayer and petition, with thanksgiving, present your requests to God. And the peace of God, which transcends all understanding, will guard your hearts and your minds in Christ Jesus. (Phil. 4:6-7, NIV)

A prayer for those living in chaos

Lord Jesus, we sit in Your arms, breathe deeply and invite You to come calm our souls. Today, chaos is swirling all around and it feels like life is out of control. Tempers are hot, patience is thin and darkness threatens to gain the upper hand. It feels as if we are being slammed against the rocks—the waves are crashing over us and we can scarcely catch our breath. So, Lord, we ask You to climb into the boat with us now and take over the helm. Please calm the storm, as only You can. And Jesus, calm *us*, as well. We pray for Your perfect peace to wash over us, quieting the turmoil. Thank You for loving us so completely and letting us know how special we are to You. We pray in the Name of the One who still calms the storms. Amen.

GOING DEEPER—GETTING PERSONAL ——————

1. Can you identify with the words, "This is not the life I signed up for!" Why or why not?

2. Taking into account your child's age and diagnosis, what causes the most chaos in your life today? Or are you experiencing a season of calm?

3. Can you recall a time or an incident in your life when you clearly felt the peace of Christ calm your storm?

CHAPTER TWO

Equipped by God:
Chosen, Trusted, Empowered

A GLIMPSE INSIDE

There are approximately seven billion people walking the earth today. And YOU are one of them! By taking a look at the sheer number of people, it stands to reason that there are hundreds of millions of moms, hundreds of millions of dads and hundreds of millions of children. How was it that your specific family came into being? Do you think it was an accident of cosmic fate that brought your family together?

Long before your children were conceived, born and welcomed into your family, God knew precisely the needs they would have. He also knew that your child—the one for whom you're reading this book—would face some daunting struggles in this world. And He knew just who your child needed to have as parents. Out of seven billion people, He chose YOU for the honor of parenting this special child. Like a beautiful jigsaw puzzle, God put your family together.

Having a child with a mental illness or emotional disorder is no small thing. It takes vast amounts of energy, patience and love to parent such a child. When the disorder or illness flares out of control, it's not unusual to find our physical, emotional, financial and spiritual resources stretched thin. We may even wonder if we're equipped to parent a child with such significant issues.

Perhaps we even wonder if God made a mistake. Did He really think we could do this and do it well? After all, there are 6.9 billion others He could have chosen to be our child's parent! Yet He chose you. He chose me. And God always equips those He chooses.

As mentioned in the introduction, I often wish I had a degree in psychology! That would certainly help me better understand my son and perhaps enable me to be a more empathetic mom. But God often equips us in ways far different than how the world equips us. In addition to our education and all the other valuable resources available to us, God delights in equipping us in very personal and unique ways—ways handpicked specifically for us.

Sometimes we need the perspective of time and distance to see the overall picture a little more clearly. Here's Lisa's story:

> When I take a step back and look at the big picture of my life, I see how God has taken the most painful pieces and put them together in such a way as to make me just the right mom for Ashley. Both of my parents died when I was in my early teens, so I needed to move in with my aunt and uncle, who lived in another state. As you can imagine, this was very traumatic, and I pretty much shut down emotionally.
>
> Thankfully, God continued to work in my life and I came to know the Lord when I was in college. When I was in my mid-twenties, I was finally able to deal with my stuff, and I experienced much emotional healing.

God blessed me with Thomas, a wonderful, godly husband. After two years of marriage we were elated with the birth of a healthy baby boy. Thomas and I were thrilled when, just a year and a half later, we found out we were expecting another baby. We eagerly anticipated our little family growing by one more! My pregnancy was uneventful and nothing seemed amiss until shortly before labor and delivery. Just days before my due date, we were devastated to discover our precious preborn baby had died in my womb. We were crushed even further when we found out I would not be able to have any more children. This was a very, very difficult time for me—for all of us.

We eventually came to accept this heartbreaking life change and decided to pursue adoption. We knew God had another child for us and eagerly went through the long adoption process. We were overjoyed when we were finally able to bring home our precious four-year-old daughter! When Ashley had been with us for just a few short months, however, we discovered she had some pretty significant needs. Ashley was eventually diagnosed with fetal alcohol syndrome and autism spectrum disorder. Ashley's growing-up years were very difficult for all of us. There was a lot of anger, lying, drama, self-injury, running away, school suspensions, etc. For a time I struggled with thinking I couldn't even do adoption "right." There were many times I was at the end of my rope. I wondered why God chose US to be the parents of this difficult child.

I thought that surely some other family could have done it so much better.

Then, when Ashley was in her teens, God gave me a glimpse of how He is able to work everything out for good. Ashley was heartbroken that she would never get to meet her birthmother and went through a time of deep grieving. I was very sad for Ashley, and I shared with her my own feelings of loss when both my parents were killed and again when our infant baby died. I could relate very well to the emotions Ashley was expressing. God, in His grace, gave me a little peek into how He had uniquely equipped me to be Ashley's mom.

Perhaps Lisa's speculation—"I thought that surely another family could have done it so much better"—reflects the hearts of many parents whose children struggle with emotional or mental health challenges. To be honest, it's a struggle I had for many years. Steve and I felt completely unprepared for the upheaval and dysfunction our family began to experience in Kyle's growing-up years. I vividly remember suggesting to God that perhaps He had made a mistake in allowing us to be Kyle's parents! I was positive another set of parents could surely do it so much better. I felt ill-prepared and unequipped to be the mom of such a challenging child.

I have a hunch I'm not alone in my thinking. As parents, we want to do the very best we can for our children. We want to love and parent them well, to bring them safely into adulthood and send them out—healthy and whole—into their futures. As idealistic young parents, we think we have a pretty good idea of what our families will look like and how this whole parenting thing will go.

Then reality strikes. We discover our child has complex issues that even our deepest love can't heal. All the parenting books in the world can't answer the questions we wrestle with deep in our hearts. Oftentimes, we're just not sure we can do this. We feel completely ill-equipped to parent a child with such difficult issues.

Henry and Virginia are parents of several children, all of whom struggle with some sort of mental or emotional disorder. Henry stated, "The growing-up years with our children were very difficult. It was like dominoes falling. One child would be diagnosed, then another and yet another." Virginia acknowledged that mental illness has affected every area of their family life—education, finances, relationships, physical health, etc. "Nothing has been left untouched."

When mental illness disrupts a child's life, parents experience the pain of feeling as if they're falling far short of providing the help their child needs. As Virginia mentioned, every area of life is affected. So when the school calls yet again, we struggle with thinking we're the ones who are failing. When our child's relationships crumble, we ache because we're powerless to hold them together. When our teenage daughter runs away, or when we discover our twenty-year-old son is using drugs, or when our child ends up in prison, we feel questioned and judged by those around us, as well as by the one looking back at us in the mirror.

And we're just not sure we can do this. Did God make a mistake in choosing us to parent this child?

We begin to believe the taunts of Satan we've all heard: "This is all YOUR fault. You've messed up your kid. You don't know what you're doing. God must be punishing you for something. You're all alone in this battle. You are weak. You are helpless. You are completely unequipped, and God really messed up by choosing YOU to be this child's parent."

So did God make a mistake? When doubts creep in, God invites you to take a closer look at your life—peering at it through His lens. God, in His infinite wisdom, has chosen *you* to be the parent of this child. He did not make a mistake. He knew it would possibly be the hardest thing He's ever asked of you—but He knows that with His help you can do it! He has equipped you well. Isaiah 45:3 tells us He has given us *"treasures hidden in the darkness—secret riches."* When you light a candle in the darkness of your circumstances, you might be surprised to find some very unique ways God has perfectly equipped YOU to be your child's mom or dad.

GAZING UP

1 Cor. 12:18b tells us, *"As it is, we see that God has carefully placed each part of the body right where he wanted it"* (MSG). Just as God has put each part of our physical body where He desires it to be, so He has put each member of the body of Christ where He wants us to be and has equipped us for the challenges He knew we would encounter.

"I am The Lord; there is no other God. I have equipped you for battle…" (Is. 45:5a, NLT).

Many days it does feel like we're in a battle, and the stakes are high. Yet God assures us He has equipped us—and is equipping us—for the battle we're in.

What does God's equipping look like? The benediction in Hebrews 13:20-21 gives us insight into this: *"Now may the God of peace…equip you with everything good for doing his will, and may he work in us what is pleasing to him, through Jesus Christ, to whom be glory for ever and ever. Amen"* (NIV).

In place of the word "equip," the KJV phrases it this way: "...[*may God] make you perfect in every good work to do his will.*"

According to *Strong's Concordance*, some of the meanings of "to make perfect" are, "to put in order, to make complete, to equip, to prepare and to perfectly join together."[1]

When God gave you a child with a mental illness or an emotional disorder, He did not make a mistake. He planned this long in advance. In addition, He not only planned and put your family together, He also planned and put you together just as He intended. He *perfectly joined together*—perfectly furnished, prepared and equipped you—with everything you would need to do His will and to be the parent of your child(ren). With His help, you are well-equipped!

In my interviews with parents, I enjoyed asking the question, "Do you feel God equipped you for this task? If so, in what way(s)?"

Some parents very honestly shared they did *not* feel equipped, especially as the struggles and challenges grew more difficult. Most, though, were able to identify some very specific ways they feel God prepared and equipped them to be the parents of a child with a mental health disorder.

Several parents openly confided *their own struggles* with abuse or mental illness—or the struggles of close family members—and how that had served to better prepare them to parent their children. Henry and Virginia, the parents mentioned above, know they better understand their children because of their own mental health issues. They readily acknowledge that God gives them strength for each day for the issues they battle. They also recognize that God has put other people in place to help them.

Sharon, a middle-aged mom of one daughter, grew up in a very volatile home and was abused physically, verbally and sexually by those she should have been able to trust. Sharon and her husband adopted their daughter, Leah, when she was six years old. Similar to Sharon's story, Leah's early years were also very horrific. Leah had been sexually abused from a very early age and was eventually removed from her home. Sharon recognizes that, because of her own abuse, she innately knows what Leah struggles with and is better equipped to understand and empathize with her daughter.

Deanna, a mom of a young son with autism spectrum disorder, related a very specific way she feels God prepared and equipped her for parenting a child with autism. "I feel that my genetics is one way God equipped me to be Evan's mom. There is a tendency toward mental illness in my family, so I understand it better than others might. I struggle with chronic depression. Sometimes I wonder if God allows these mental illnesses to run in families because we can say, 'I get it,' when dealing with our own children."

Vanessa's daughter, Sierra, has a diagnosis of bipolar disorder, generalized anxiety disorder and sensory processing disorder. Sierra experienced her first inpatient hospitalization at the age of seven. However, living with and loving someone with a mental illness was not new to Vanessa. "My mom also struggles with bipolar disorder. Now I see the other side of the coin, since I have a daughter with bipolar disorder. I better understand my daughter because of my life with my mom."

Many parents recognize that their educational backgrounds, life experiences or personality traits have equipped them with the perseverance, strength and patience necessary to parent a child with such significant issues. Connie said, "I'm proactive. I'm a strong advocate for my kids, and I don't give up on getting what they need. If I feel strongly about something, I really go to work on it! I've been given an inquisitive mind; I love to read and do research. Plus, I have low blood pressure and don't get terribly excited about things! All of these things have helped me be the mom Will needs."

Cyndi believes God equipped her to be the mother of a child with a brain disorder by how He created her personality. "I'm a nurturer and caregiver by nature. I've always had a huge heart for the underdog and the marginalized. I definitely see how God has used those traits to help me be a gentler, more understanding mom to Peter."

Glenn and Ella, whose son is now in his late thirties, acknowledged that life has been difficult with Kent. Ella related, "We've experienced a lot of highs and lows throughout life. At the beginning, we certainly didn't feel equipped to be Kent's parents. But now, looking back over the years, I definitely see ways God prepared and provided for us. I am a very patient person by nature, and I'm a teacher by trade. I've learned how to remain very calm around Kent. I recognize his moods and am sensitive to what he needs." Glenn added, "God has blessed us with a strong, healthy marriage. He has also blessed us financially. I've been able to provide well for our family, and we've had the resources necessary to provide Kent with the best possible care."

Russ and Leslie have adopted several children out of the foster care system. When asked how they feel they've been equipped for such a challenging life, Leslie stated that her education degree has been very helpful. Her husband, Russ, has a gentle, empathetic nature—and both stated they simply love kids! Russ told me, "I think it's our mission in life to be their parents."

We've looked at several creative, personal ways God fashioned and made us, equipping us with the necessary tools, skills, life experiences and personalities to be just the parents our children need. In the midst of the variety, however, there was one overriding and constant theme: Most of the parents expressed, in one way or another, the importance of their *faith in God*. There was a deep recognition within these parents that they could not be doing this without God's help. Even though they could pinpoint several specific ways God had equipped them, they knew their relationship with Christ was of upmost importance. He remained their strong and steady lifeline each time the chaos threatened to overwhelm them.

Indeed, our relationship with God not only equips us, but also sustains and strengthens us as we traverse through life. Our path is often bumpy and difficult, but God's divine power is available to supply us with whatever we need.

Our own resources will never be adequate. Our own strength, determination and natural talents will always fall a bit short. The Apostle Paul recognized this as well and reminded us, *"It is not that we…are qualified to do anything on our own. Our qualification comes from God. He has enabled us…" (2 Cor. 3:5-6a, NLT).*

There are many ways God enables and empowers us as we journey through difficult days and trying times with our children. Two fail-proof ways, however, rise to the surface: 1) allowing His Word to come to life within us; and 2) discovering the power of prayer.

The first powerful tool God has given us is His written Word. He loves when we dive into the Scriptures! It's packed full of beautiful promises written very specifically for His children. If we barely dip our toes in, we will miss so much. In order to best parent our children, we need to discover His words of hope, His promises of peace and His declarations of love. To be well-equipped with His strength, we need to be infused with the richness of His Word.

The second amazing tool with which God equips us is prayer. Daily He invites us to make a holy exchange with Him—our burdens for His abundance. God isn't looking for long, eloquent prayers. He encourages us to come to Him very simply and honestly, handing Him our weaknesses, our fears, our inadequacies. In exchange, He provides us with the energy, wisdom and strength we need for the day—for that moment.

Author Philip Yancey noted that Jesus Himself relied on prayer to equip Him for His work: "Jesus counted on prayer as a source of strength that equipped him to carry out a partnership with God the Father on earth. Jesus freely admitted his dependence: the Son can do nothing by himself; he can do only what he sees his Father doing."[2]

As you struggle with daily challenges and burdens, may His words seal your reliance on Him, equipping and empowering you to do the next thing: *"I can do all things [which He has called me to do] through Him who strengthens and empowers me [to fulfill His purpose—I am self-sufficient in Christ's sufficiency; I am ready for anything and equal to anything through Him who infuses me with inner strength and confident peace.]" (Phil. 4:13, AMP).*

Additional Scripture to meditate on

I can do all things through Christ who strengthens me.
(Phil. 4:13, NKJV)

Praise be the Lord, to God our Savior, who daily bears our burdens. (Psalm 68:19, NIV)

His divine power has given us everything we need for a godly life through our knowledge of him who called us by his own glory and goodness. (2 Peter 1:3, NIV)

And the Holy Spirit helps us in our weakness. For example, we don't know what God wants us to pray for. But the Holy Spirit prays for us with groanings that cannot be expressed in words.

And the Father who knows all hearts knows what the Spirit is saying, for the Spirit pleads for us believers in harmony with God's own will. (Romans 8:26-27, NLT)

A prayer of blessing and equipping

Dear Jesus, thank You for how You put our family together. You've given us an awesome—and sometimes scary—job to do. You've called us to be the mom or dad of a child who struggles with a brain disorder. Whether our child is young and still living under our roof or is grown and living away, we're very aware of how much we need Your strength and grace to parent well. Thank You for carrying us in Your arms each day. Thank You for infusing us with Your strength and empowering us with everything we need to fulfill Your purposes.

We open our hands and heart and receive Your blessing: "*Now may the God of peace, who through the blood of the eternal covenant brought back from the dead our Lord Jesus, that great Shepherd of the sheep, equip you with everything good for doing his will, and may he work in us what is pleasing to him, through Jesus Christ, to whom be glory for ever and ever (Heb. 13:20-21).*" Amen.

GOING DEEPER—GETTING PERSONAL ———————

1. In what unique, personal ways has God equipped you to be the parent of your child?

2. With what lies has Satan taunted you as you've parented your child? How would you refute those lies?

3. What holy exchange is God inviting you to make with Him today? What burdens are you carrying? What do you desire from God in exchange for your burdens?

CHAPTER THREE

Face to Face with a "No" From God: Our Disappointment— His Grace

A GLIMPSE INSIDE

The sadness, disappointment and emotional pain emanating from this hurting couple was palpable. "We simply don't understand why God won't heal our daughter. We know He is able. We love to collect stories of miraculous healings—healings from every sort of illness, accident and trauma imaginable. We know it wouldn't be too hard for God to miraculously heal our daughter of her major depression. We just can't figure out why He keeps saying 'no' to her healing."

One attribute of Jesus that is profoundly touching is His compassionate desire to heal. The Gospels[1] brim with the best stories of miraculous healings ever written! As we study these Biblical accounts, we're privileged to pull up a chair and take a firsthand look at Jesus in the flesh as He lived and walked on earth. It's enjoyable to meditate on these stories and imagine what it would have been like to live in an ancient village where Jesus spent time. These words paint such a tender, compassionate picture of Jehovah-Rapha, the Lord who heals: *"As the sun went down that evening, people throughout the village brought sick family members to Jesus. No matter what their diseases were, the touch of his hand healed every one. Many were possessed by demons; and the demons came out at his command, shouting, 'You are the Son of God!'"* (*Luke 4:40-41a, NLT*).

What a beautiful portrait of Jesus' love. Imagine the relief so many experienced as they brought someone they loved to Jesus. Imagine the joy and delight of seeing their loved one fully healed!

What, then, are we to do with passages like John 5:1-15? In this story, we read how Jesus healed a man who had been ill for thirty-eight long years. Day after day, year after year this poor man existed under a covered colonnade beside what was called the Pool of Bethesda. We're told that, "here a great number of disabled people used to lie—the blind, the lame, the paralyzed." They were waiting for the water to be stirred, knowing they would be miraculously healed if immersed at just the right time. One day, Jesus happened to be walking nearby and noticed this man lying on one of the porches. Jesus asked him an intriguing question: "Do you want to get well?" The invalid must have looked at Jesus with surprise to be asked such an obvious question. He explained that he was never able to get into the water when it was stirred, as someone else always got in ahead of him. Jesus looked at him and simply said, "Get up! Pick up your mat and walk." And just like that, the man was healed! Amazing!

But, back up a bit.

The story tells us a great number of sick and disabled people were lying there, waiting for the opportunity to be healed. What about them? Why did Jesus leave a multitude of people behind that day—still sick, still broken, still waiting? Why didn't Jesus heal everyone lying around the pool? Jesus was right there—in their very midst. He had the power to heal them all, just as He had the power to heal the one. Imagine the bewilderment and disappointment the others must have felt as they watched Jesus walk away...leaving them lying helplessly on their mats. Why didn't Jesus heal them?

These probing questions tend to scrape the scabs off our own disappointments. Perhaps we wonder why our child has not been healed—why God has continued to say "no" or "not yet" to our repeated requests for restoration. Our hearts bleed and ache with sadness that our child is still part of this "great number" and continues to suffer the effects of mental illness.

If we dare to be honest, there are times that reading through the Gospel accounts of Jesus' healing miracles leaves us feeling somewhat disillusioned. Jesus healed so many. He willingly, compassionately and completely healed people with all sorts of diseases, including those possessed by demons. He even raised dead people to life. Jesus often told the people it was because of their faith that they were healed. Other times He made it clear that it was the faith of a parent or friend that touched Jesus' heart and brought about healing. In other instances, we read that Jesus chose to heal and restore simply because of His compassion and there is no mention made of anyone's faith.

Perhaps many of these stories are highlighted and underlined in our own Bibles. Stories of Jesus' compassion and healing power touch our hearts and motivate our faith, reminding us of the dynamic power found in even mustard-seed-sized faith. But sometimes this is also where hurt and confusion begin to set in. Perhaps you can say with all honesty, "I *do* have a lot of faith. I do pray boldly and believe that with God, all things are possible. I have even seen healing miracles happen." Yet your child continues to struggle in most all areas of his or her life. And that brings stabbing pain to your heart.

One mom quietly whispered her pain, as if fearful of being over-heard, "I've often pleaded with God to heal my daughter's mind and emotions, to take away her anxieties and bring her some freedom. I've implored God to give her one or two good friends—ones who would treat her with respect and kindness. I've asked God to help her find and keep a job, to provide her with employment to fill her days and give her satisfaction. None of these things would be hard for God to do. Yet in the midst of so many other answered prayers, God seems silent on these. And it hurts. To be honest, there are times I feel sad and disappointed with the way God chooses to work."

Parent after parent echoed these sentiments. Many spoke of feeling disappointed with God, frustrated with Him and even angry at Him. They long for God to heal their child, to take away the turmoil and chaos that creates discord in their homes and to mend broken relationships. "Why won't God heal my son/my daughter?" was a common query. "How long do we have to deal with this chaos? I just don't understand. What is God doing?"

Tracy, a mom of two adult children with mental health disorders, remembers a time she struggled intensely with God. "The infancy of both of our children was very challenging. They had significant sleep issues, and I lived in a state of constant exhaustion. The dynamics between the two kids has always been awful, and we were typically perplexed about how to best parent them. Nothing we said or did seemed to have any positive effect on them. Family counseling wasn't successful, nor was the individual therapy we sought for our children. In fact, one therapist straight-out told us, 'I just don't know what to do with Belinda anymore.' We were overwhelmed much of the time. Then, when our son, Braden, was eleven, he was hospitalized and diagnosed with severe depression. It was at this point that I experienced a major faith crisis. I was very angry at God for a while. I had no use for a God who would do this to His children. I especially felt that church was unbearably pleasant, and it was hard for me to attend."

Bruce and Rhonda, whose two young adult children struggle with deep psychological brokenness, shared their honest emotions with me. "We do struggle with disappointment and even some anger at God. Life is just hard. Our expectations were so high, and the reality is so different. It's hard how everything in our lives came apart as our kids got older. We get nothing from them. No love. No affirmation. No respect. It's as if they almost hate us."

Other parents spoke of feeling a deep sadness about the things God has allowed to continue, instead of bringing healing to their child and relief to their situation.

Kimberly stated, "Yes, my husband and I are sometimes sad and disappointed with how life turned out. We certainly didn't sign up for this, and neither did our daughter, Skylar. There are times I find myself questioning God and asking Him, 'Why?' Why did He allow such horrible abuse to scar my child? There are times I say, 'I can't believe this is my daughter's life. I can't believe this is MY life.'"

Carol shared, "I'm sad that life is not easier for Max. It hurts my heart that he is not able to be part of a 'normal' life. Others seem to have it all together. It's hard to see Max struggle. He wants to be with others and to have friends, but he just doesn't know how. I sometimes ask Jesus, 'Why us? Why Max?' My siblings and friends all have more typical kids, and they all seem to be doing well in school, sports, etc. Life is hard, but I simply try to find the beauty in where we are."

If we linger here, the questions arise and doubts begin to swirl. Why doesn't Jesus heal my son or daughter? Is my faith not enough? Where is Jesus' compassion for my child? Doesn't He see us? Doesn't He care? Why is God so silent?

Hard questions. Heartfelt laments.

What are we to do with our disappointment, sadness and anger in the face of repeated "no's" from God? How do we process this?

GAZING UP

The very fact that you're reading this book makes it likely you were given a "no" or "not yet" by God. Your child continues to live with an emotional or mental illness, and your family continues to experience periodic upheaval. Many of your hopes and dreams have been dashed. On the surface, we understand life is hard. Sin did—and does—wreak extensive havoc in this world. Jesus reminded His disciples of this very thing in John 16:33: *"Here on earth you will have many trials and sorrows. But take heart, because I have overcome the world" (NLT)*. So we know that, on this side of heaven, there will be sorrow, suffering, illnesses, trials and heartache; after all, we live in a fallen, broken world. We understand that more than we ever thought we would.

What's disillusioning, though, is when we page through the Gospels and read story after story of Jesus healing those who came to Him—yet our child remains ill, broken. What we struggle with is when we read verse after verse about "asking, seeking and knocking" and we're promised that "all these things will be given to us"[2]—but we *haven't* received what we've asked for, even though we've asked in faith. Or we come across verses like, "You have not because you ask not"[3]—but our hearts cry out that we *have* asked for our child's healing, for our family's restoration, and for relief from the chaos over and over, but to no avail.

What are we to make of these promises? Is there something we're missing here? When God clearly and unequivocally answers our requests with a "no" or "not yet," perhaps it's time to readjust our focus. When we're struggling with the pain of a "no"-answered prayer, it's time to take our eyes off our problems and look fully at the face of Jesus. He looks at us with love and understanding while patiently reminding us of a few things.

First, the ways of God are always higher than ours. His thoughts are nothing like our thoughts, and His ways are far beyond anything we could imagine.[4] God wants us to trust Him. He knows what He's doing. He always has a plan.

Second, God's ways are often mysterious. God's Word gives us an amazingly full picture of His character, but He does not need to answer to us. He retains the right to mystery. God holds the power of life and death, and in faith and trust *we* yield to *Him*. Ecclesiastes 11:5 poetically reminds us, *"Just as you cannot understand the path of the wind or the mystery of a tiny baby growing in his mother's womb, so you cannot understand the activity of God, who does all things"* (NLT).

Third, each time we're told "no," we're given another opportunity to experience the fullness of God's grace. In our mind's eye, each time God says "no," we think He's holding out on us—snatching something away that we so desperately need or want. In His eyes, however, He's offering us the incredible gift of His grace. Indeed, every painful "no" we receive from God, comes wrapped in the warmth of His grace. His all-surpassing, generous grace is given in direct proportion to our needs. The more profound our need, the more abundant His grace.

Jesus whispers to us the same energy-infusing words with which He strengthened the Apostle Paul: *"My grace is sufficient for you, for my power is made perfect in weakness" (2 Cor. 12:9, NIV).* Jesus' grace *is* sufficient. It is enough for whatever disappointment we face.

So many brave parents can give affirmation to the sufficient grace of Jesus, even in—especially in—the worst life has to offer.

Kimberly's adopted daughter, Skylar, has lived through a nightmare of incest, beatings and rejection. The trauma she suffered left deep scars, and her life continues to be very messy. Kimberly has prayed long and hard for her daughter's healing, yet understands that the brokenness of life and the horrendous choices of others have likely damaged her daughter's emotional health permanently. Kimberly is very aware, though, of what the sufficiency of Jesus looks like in her life. She said, "God has carried me through. I could not have shouldered this by myself. Only by the grace of God have I survived and gotten through this. God has carried me—and Skylar—all the way, and I trust He won't put us down now."

Ben and Terri, too, know what it's like to intercede and implore God over and over for a child's healing. Their adult daughter, Stacia, struggles greatly with her mental illness. She's working hard to remain stable. She is generally compliant with taking her medication, exercises regularly and tries to eat well. However, from time to time she relapses, resulting in deep emotional pain—not only for Stacia, but also for Ben and Terri. Yet they have seen and experienced the loving sufficiency of God in many ways. Even though, for now, God has chosen not to heal their daughter, Ben recounts how he has seen many answers to prayer. "God has provided jobs for Stacia when needed. He's also provided the help she's needed, such as adequate hospitalization, a good therapist and life-saving medication." Terri added, "Each day when I wake up I ask God to be with me. God knows I love Him, even though there are days I feel very angry with Him. Yet I think just the fact I have the energy and desire to get out of bed most days shows me He's there for me, helping me, loving me."

God's sufficient grace comes wrapped in all shapes and sizes and shows up in a variety of ways. On some days, God's grace is His hand gently waking us up, giving us the courage to throw off the covers and get out of bed. His grace encourages us to take His outstretched hand, reminding us He's walking through the pain with us. At other times, it's His still, small voice prompting us to trust Him, even in the unimaginable. Sometimes, God's grace comes packaged as a dream or a vision, giving us a vivid reminder of His compassionate love for us.

Kathryn recalls a vision she received when she was in a very painful place in life: "When Nick was a baby, I remember a strong impression I received one day as I was lying down, resting. Craig and I were having problems in our marriage, and we were separated. At that point, Craig was allowed supervised visits with Nick. I remember thinking of how difficult the past years had been. I knew I had to give them to God. As I did, I had a vision of Jesus giving me some beautiful flowers. I knew then that somehow God would transform these painful years into something beautiful."

The amazing, sufficient grace of Jesus! When we surrender our dreams, our desires, our humility, our weaknesses—our very lives—on His altar, He offers us a beautiful exchange.

> *He takes hold of our weary, weak emotions and offers us His life-giving strength.*
> *He loosens our white-knuckled grasp for control and offers to take over the reins.*
> *He kneels next to us in our ugly, broken pride and offers us the gift of humility.*

He listens to our rants, rages and anger, and offers us His
    forgiveness, peace and calm.
He hears our cries of fear and panic and offers us a peace that
    surpasses understanding.
He understands our disappointment and frustration and offers
    us deeply rooted joy.
He takes the empty vessels of our lives and fills us with His over-
    flowing, all-sufficient grace.

Are you willing to trust God, even if the healing never comes?
The tender love and abundant grace of Jesus is available to carry us
through every disappointment. His grace is enough. *He* is enough.

Additional Scripture to meditate on

*Are God's consolations not enough for you, words spoken gently
to you? (Job 15:11, NIV)*

*"For my thoughts are not your thoughts,
    neither are your ways my ways,"
declares the* LORD.
*"As the heavens are higher than the earth,
    so are my ways higher than your ways
    and my thoughts than your thoughts." (Isaiah 55:8-9, NIV)*

*Because of the extravagance of those revelations, and so I
wouldn't get a big head, I was given the gift of a handicap to
keep me in constant touch with my limitations. Satan's angel did
his best to get me down; what he in fact did was push me to my
knees. No danger then of walking around high and mighty! At*

*first I didn't think of it as a gift, and begged God to remove it.
Three times I did that, and then he told me,*

*My grace is enough; it's all you need.
My strength comes into its own in your weakness.*

*Once I heard that, I was glad to let it happen. I quit focusing on
the handicap and began appreciating the gift. It was a case of
Christ's strength moving in on my weakness. Now I take limitations in stride, and with good cheer, these limitations that cut me
down to size — abuse, accidents, opposition, bad breaks. I just let
Christ take over! And so the weaker I get, the stronger I become.*
(2 Cor. 12:7-10, MSG)

A prayer for God's sufficient grace

Jesus, in our vulnerability we whisper, "Your grace is sufficient for
me today. Your power is made perfect in weakness." Show us Your
grace, Lord. Entrust us with Your power. We know we can't do this
on our own. This situation is too big and we're too tired, too weak. We
find ourselves face to face with a "no" from You, and we're frightened,
fearful and worried. Sometimes we struggle with anger—at our children, our situation, ourselves—even at You. Yet You calmly remind us
time and again, "My grace is sufficient. It's all you need. My power is
made perfect in weakness." Thank You, dear Jesus, for the sufficiency
of Your grace. It's the only way we can truly get through our days
with any semblance of victory. Thank You for the great exchange
You continually offer. You take all our weakness, pain, sadness and
disappointment and offer us the beautiful gift of Yourself. You are
enough, Jesus. You are always and forever enough. We love You. Amen.

GOING DEEPER—GETTING PERSONAL ———————

1. What disappointing "no's" have you received from God?

2. How have you experienced God walking with you on this journey? Can you identify ways His grace has carried you as you've struggled with your child's mental illness?

3. In 2 Cor. 12:7-10 (from the MSG, written on page 37), the Apostle Paul exclaimed, in regard to his weaknesses, "I just let Christ take over!" How easy is this to do? How do you see Christ's power and strength being "made perfect" in the weakest areas of your life?

CHAPTER FOUR

Grief:
Our Lifelong Roller
Coaster Ride

A GLIMPSE INSIDE

Carolyn, a soft-spoken woman in her seventies, shared with me her long-traveled journey on the path of grief:

> I remember so well the joy and excitement we felt in bringing our little daughter home. She had been in the foster care system, but now she was coming home, to our home—to her forever family! I also remember with aching clarity the stabbing grief in my heart when our daughter began to exhibit some very difficult behaviors. Regardless of how we tried to bond with her, she pushed us away. In public she would act appropriately toward us, but at home she spit at us, hit us, cursed us and lied to us. She continued to be defiant, manipulative and hateful throughout her growing-up years.

She is now well into adulthood and continues to make incredibly poor and damaging choices. Our relationship is pretty much estranged. The only time I hear from her is when she needs something. Each time she calls, I'm plunged into grief for a few days. A counselor once told me, "You grieve for what is, what could have been and what never will be."

As this precious, wounded mom shared her hurt, the words of Simeon the prophet came to mind. When Mary and Joseph brought their holy infant son to the temple to present Him to the Lord, Simeon immediately took notice and joyfully scooped the baby boy into his arms. After he praised God, Simeon blessed the new parents and their tiny baby. Then he turned and spoke directly to Mary. He prophesied that people would either joyfully accept her son or painfully oppose and reject him. He ended his prophecy with these troubling words, *"And a sword will pierce your own soul, too" (NIV).*[1]

As moms and dads of a child with a psychiatric illness or deep emotional brokenness, we've often felt as if a sword has, indeed, pierced our hearts. We think back to our child's infancy—or when we first welcomed this precious one into our lives—and we remember our soaring hopes and dreams. As we reflect on how our child's life is playing out, however, we often feel the deep thrust of the sword. We never expected this—this aching grief that never ends.

We grieve for what our child has experienced, and we grieve for what they've been denied. We grieve the choices they've made, and we grieve the choices that have been withheld. We grieve the ways they've been publicly mocked and ridiculed, and we grieve for how they've been overlooked and misunderstood. We grieve that few see the beauty that is often hidden under the darkness of mental illness.

For many of us, this grief began very early in our child's life. Carolyn shared that the first time she and her husband suspected their daughter, Wendy, had a psychological disorder was when their little girl was barely out of infancy. With growing dismay, they realized their one-year-old child simply did not care whether she pleased anyone or not. She had no empathy for others, pushed everyone away, had horrible temper tantrums and was very aggressive. This pattern continued throughout her life, and Carolyn's daughter was eventually diagnosed with antisocial personality disorder.

For others, the grief hit hard when mental illness seemed to come out of nowhere and strike their child. Tim and Meredith's son, Chance, seemed to undergo a total personality change during his early years of college. This kind young man went from amicable to angry, seemingly overnight. He was hostile and arrogant, wrought with grandiose ideas, thinking he was superior and invincible. Eventually Chance was hospitalized, diagnosed with bipolar disorder and put on medication. He is back in school and doing well, but his parents continue to worry and wonder what his future holds. The grief continues for them.

In my interviews with parents, I asked the question, "What are some specific things you grieve, especially in regard to your child?" Their answers seemed to uncover two themes. The first is that our grief is *multifaceted*. There is a wide variety of "deaths" we experience that tend to pierce our hearts and cause us grief. Second, our grief is *never-ending*. When we experience any loss in life and find ourselves plunged into grief, we often talk about "going through" it, as if grief is a tunnel from which we will eventually emerge. Unfortunately, the grief we experience—as parents of children with severe and chronic psychological disorders—is one which we never completely walk through and leave behind. Instead of a tunnel, our particular brand of grief seems to be a never-ending roller coaster ride. We climb aboard this roller coaster at the onset of our child's psychological and emotional struggles, and we ride this coaster throughout their lives and ours. When our children are functioning well and enjoying a period of stability, we find the ride to be manageable—even pleasant. But when their illness becomes symptomatic and psychosis rears its ugly head, we find ourselves, once again, plunging to the depths.

Grief.

We grieve deeply for our children and the incredible difficulties they endure in life, and we also grieve for ourselves. We grieve the death of a dream—the dream of what we thought our families would look like and the lives we thought our children would live. We grieve marriages that did not survive and friendships that have gone on without us. Our other children grieve as well. The white-hot poker of grief stabs their questioning hearts as they recognize the dysfunction in their homes and long for "normal" (more on siblings is included in Chapter 14).

Whether our children show signs of emotional brokenness as very young children or much later in their lives, the next season of grief seems to be waiting just around the bend.

Grief at the beginning of the journey

Parents whose children were adopted from abusive and broken homes grieve for the loss of innocence their children experienced at a very young age. Gloria adopted her little girl at the age of four. Cadence had been severely abused (physically and sexually) in her infant and toddler years. The trauma she experienced at the hands of others scarred her in unfathomable ways—not just physically, but emotionally as well. Gloria aches deeply for her daughter. She especially grieves Cadence's loss of innocence at such an early age. She regrets that this innocence can never be regained, and she struggles with how this loss has forever changed her daughter. She sees how it has adversely affected all relationships for Cadence. Most of all, Gloria grieves that Cadence cannot accept her great value in God's eyes. Cadence is very vulnerable and often acts out in destructive ways.

Marcy and Travis grieve the early-life experiences of their son, Jacob, as well. Jacob had been in and out of foster homes for most of his early years. He also spent time on the streets or in shelters with his biological mom when he was in her custody. He witnessed and experienced things no young child should ever have to endure. Marcy laments, "Jacob experienced hunger, neglect and abuse. As a result, he is very difficult to handle. He is often fearful, yet also very angry. He is extremely defiant, has severe rages and is prone to violence." Marcy continues, "I grieve for Jacob—for the horrible things he endured in his early life. I grieve his lack of understanding about a future for himself. At this point, he cannot even envision a future. And I grieve for how this has forever changed our family dynamics. Our family has struggled in countless ways because of Jacob. Our teenage daughter is often embarrassed by how Jacob acts out and says things like, 'I just want to be a normal family.'"

Rob and Susanna grieve deeply for their son, Mac. As a little boy, Mac witnessed the violent death of his birthmother. Now in his twenties, Mac has been diagnosed with childhood PTSD, due to his early-childhood trauma. They grieve how this trauma damaged and scarred him emotionally, and they agonize over the dark path he seems drawn to. They are sad that others don't try to understand him and about how he is so often treated with contempt and disrespect.

Russ and Leslie grieve that Jillian wasn't loved by her birth family. She was severely neglected and eventually abandoned. They grieve for the deep impact this early neglect had on their young daughter and for how she continues to struggle to have a sense of belonging.

Grief during the adolescent and teenage years

The adolescent and teenage years can be difficult and trying for all children and parents, but these years are especially challenging for those who struggle with a brain disorder. Many of our children do not have proper filters in place. Their behaviors are off-putting, and perhaps even threatening, to their peers. Our children may be invisible, isolated, lonely; they may be misunderstood and misjudged by their teachers and classmates.

Not only are these years painful for our children, but we often find ourselves saddened by them as well. We wistfully long for our kids to fit in, to have one or two close friends, to be able to enjoy their childhood. So when we see our kids shunned, made fun of and pushed away, it brings us into another season of grief.

Anna is sad that her son, Lucas, doesn't have any close friends. Even though his ADHD is not severe, he still struggles with behaviors his classmates find strange and odd. Anna occasionally is able to find a classmate to come play with Lucas, but the invitations are never reciprocated. Anna aches for her son and the loneliness he feels.

Vanessa, whose daughter, Sierra, has a diagnosis of bipolar disorder, also grieves that her daughter has no friends. "Sierra wants friends, but is unable to maintain friendships. She's never invited to birthday parties or sleepovers. Since you can't 'see' her illness on the outside, others just don't understand. I hurt for Sierra."

Rhonda grieves that her teenage daughter, Bri, is missing out on life. Brianna struggles with severe depression and anxiety and is choosing to live life from the safety of their home. It breaks Rhonda's heart that Bri has no friends, except those she meets online. It's difficult to see her daughter living the life of a recluse. "Bri's fears and anxieties are making her world so incredibly small," sighs Rhonda. "It just all makes me sad."

Grief and the young adult years

As our children become young adults, new struggles often ensue. Some parents are relieved that their children, with supports in place, are able to successfully leave home, go to college, or perhaps find a job and begin a career. Many other parents, however, are saddened that their children long to launch out, but emotionally are not capable of doing so with any degree of success. Many parents find their young adult children completely unable to function effectively in the adult world. Life becomes infinitely more challenging for those parents whose children continue making poor and destructive choices. It's especially difficult for parents whose children—now adults—find themselves in trouble with the law.

Indeed, for parents with young adult children who have severe psychological disorders, their roller coaster ride with grief is far from over.

Connie is saddened by the fact that her twenty-year-old son, Will, is not able to realize his dreams. Will longs to get his driver's license and would love to go to college to get an IT degree. She grieves the emotional pain Will deals with all the time—the isolation, the loneliness, the panic. "I hurt that Will lives such an isolated, lonely life. This is very hard to see and deal with on a daily basis."

Terri likens her daughter's struggle with mental illness to a death. "When Stacia experienced her first psychotic episode and was given the diagnosis of bipolar disorder, it felt like a death. Stacia is very private and doesn't want anyone to know about her mental illness, so very few people are aware of what we're going through. I have a friend who recently lost her husband to cancer, and I saw how everyone rallied around her. She gets so much support, so much help. We're struggling just as much, but since no one knows, no one can help. I grieve every day for my daughter—for all she lost, and for all we've lost."

Henry and Virginia struggle with the fact that their young adult children, who live with a variety of emotional and mental illnesses, are so different than their nephews and nieces. "Our nephews and nieces all seem to live such normal lives. They are able to work and function well in society. They're getting married, having children; they're NOT getting arrested. Our children's lives are starkly different. They will always need our help or the help of others in order to make it. It's just all so very tiring."

The grief continues into the adult years

I had the privilege of talking with several older parents whose children are well into adulthood. At the time of these interviews, my own son was just stepping into his adult years, and it was a stark reminder for me that mental illness doesn't dissolve with age. There will likely always be some burdens that we, as parents, carry well into our senior years. Depending on our child's struggles, they may continue to need our help and support—or that of others—for the rest of their lives. The system, however, is capable of providing only so much help. And regardless of what public supports are available, the system has no *emotional* ties to our children. The familial bond we began with our children in their earliest years is never completely severed, even for those parents whose children choose to break ties with them. Because of this innate bond, pain and grief are companions that likely will come calling from time to time even throughout our "golden" years.

Lillian, a widow in her early seventies, will occasionally acknowledge the grief she feels over the loss of her son, Jay. Jay, now in his forties, has struggled with severe mental illness most of his life. He is estranged not only from his mom, brothers and sister, but also from his children (from three failed marriages). Lillian is aware that Jay is addicted to meth and other drugs, but she knows very little else about him. Most of the time no one knows where he is staying or how he is eking out a living. Lillian told me she fears someone knocking on her door someday with news of his death. She wishes Jay would be arrested; then she would at least know where he was and that he would be getting some semblance of help. Lillian readily agrees that grief has accompanied her for as long as Jay has struggled. She told me that even though the grief has abated through the years, there are situations that still trigger it from time to time. Having lived through the experience of losing her husband a few years ago, Lillian told me, "I have found there are worse things than death. The sense of having lost my son—even though he is alive—brings a very difficult, confusing kind of grief."

Carolyn, whose daughter Wendy is now forty-two, grieves that they have no relationship. "She has totally shut me out, and it's very painful. I haven't seen her for over two and a half years. She did recently call me to ask for money, but slammed the phone down when I told her I couldn't help her. I was plunged into deep grief for days after that. It just never ends."

Carolyn also shared her concern over her daughter's spiritual health. "I grieve that, as far as I can tell, Wendy is not a Christian. But I realize that only the Lord knows her heart. Even though there's no evidence of a relationship with Christ, I hold on to the fact that Christ knows and sees her heart. He totally understands mental illness."

Kathryn grieves for her son Nick, age thirty-four, who has a diagnosis of bipolar disorder and generalized anxiety disorder. Because of his high anxiety, he's been unable to hold down a job, even though he was able to complete his college degree at age twenty-eight. Nick spends some time volunteering at a hospital, but his anxieties make it hard for him to do even that on a regular basis. Since Nick's illness didn't flare up until his late teens, Kathryn vividly remembers the shock and grief that came after Nick's first manic-depressive episode. Kathryn told me, "I remember at one time very specifically grieving the loss of a normal life. I continue to grieve my dreams and Nick's dreams. I grieve the life he will never have—the life he thought he'd have."

GAZING UP

Grief. It's a companion we can't quite seem to shake on our journey through life with our child. One mother shared that her therapist spoke of *anticipatory grief*—the knowing that another crisis will likely be emerging sometime, somewhere just over the horizon. There may be seasons, perhaps even years, when the roller coaster ride is smooth and manageable, perhaps even enjoyable. Then inexplicably the bottom falls out. We receive an email from our child's teacher, or an angry, upsetting phone call from another parent, a knock on the door from a police officer, or a disheartening call from our adult child reporting yet another job lost or another relationship broken. Once again our child's mental illness has flared up and the sword of grief sinks deep. Once again we find the roller coaster of life plunging rapidly downhill, and we're in the front row.

But as children of a compassionate Father, we need NEVER ride this roller coaster of grief and sadness alone.

One of the hidden blessings of grief is that it always invites us to seek the arms of the perfect Comforter. God knew how deeply His children would struggle with sadness while on earth, so He went to great lengths to reveal and establish His identity as the consummate Comforter. Throughout Scripture, all three Persons of the Trinity are identified as One who comforts. A beautiful passage relating the comfort of God the Father is found in 2 Cor. 1:3-4: *"Praise be to the God and Father of our Lord Jesus Christ, the Father of compassion and the God of all comfort, who comforts us in all our troubles..." (NIV)*. In the Gospels, we read several accounts of Jesus as Comforter in how He related to His disciples and other friends throughout His time on earth.[2] We're also told that the Holy Spirit is our Comforter—One who is with us always. As Jesus prepared His disciples for His death, resurrection and ascension, He comforted them by promising to send them the gift of the Holy Spirit. Jesus said, *"And I will ask the Father, and He will give you another Helper (Comforter, Advocate, Intercessor—Counselor, Strengthener, Standby), to be with you forever..." (John 14:16, AMP)*.

Countless passages in the Old Testament hold beautiful messages of comfort as well. The poetic words of Psalm 56:8 wrap warmly around us with this encouraging promise: *"You've kept track of my every toss and turn through the sleepless nights, each tear entered in your ledger, each ache written in your book" (MSG)*.

Jesus keeps track of every sorrow, every tear, every toss and turn of a sleepless night. He has lovingly collected each tear we've ever shed for our child, for ourselves, for the loss of so many dreams. Perhaps this tunnel of grief is one from which we'll never completely emerge. But we are not traveling the valley alone. Jesus understands our sadness and grieves with us. He holds us close and patiently listens to our sighs and complaints. He never irritably tells us to just "get over it" or "snap out of it."

Jesus also promises to redeem our grief and turn it to joy. As we will explore in Chapter 10, "When Satan Intends Evil," we grieve with hope, knowing that someday, everything will be made new. We also know that, in the here and now, God uses our pain to shape our character and help us grow. We see how He often uses our most painful experiences to help others as they walk through their own difficult trials.

The comfort of Jesus will never let us down. He holds us in His arms when we're too weak, tired and sad to take one more step. One brave mom poignantly stated, "I can't believe I'm surviving this pain, but I'm learning to rely on God day by day. Now I know what it truly means to need Jesus. I find myself clinging to His promises—clinging to Him."

Indeed, the only way through our valleys of heartache is by walking right through them, one step at a time, hand in hand with Jesus. *"Even though I walk through the darkest valley, I will not be afraid, for you are close beside me. Your rod and your staff protect and comfort me"* (Psalm 23:4, NLT).

When the sword of grief plunges deep, simply rest. Let Jesus hold you. Spend time sitting quietly in His presence, allowing His promises to revive and refresh your aching soul. He will carry you through this season of sadness. He promises.

"Praise the Lord; praise God my Savior!

For each day he carries us in his arms" (Psalm 68:19, NLT).

Additional Scripture to meditate on

Listen to me...
I have cared for you since you were born.
Yes, I carried you before you were born.
I will be your God throughout your lifetime —
until your hair is white with age.
I made you, and I will care for you.
I will carry you along and save you. (Isaiah 46:3a-4, NLT)

Now let Your unfailing love be my comfort,
in keeping with Your promise to Your servant.
(Ps. 119:76, VOICE)

Blessed are those who mourn, for they will be comforted.
(Matt.5:4, NIV)

The Lord is close to the brokenhearted
and saves those who are crushed in spirit. (Ps. 34:18, NIV)

A prayer for those living in a season of grief

Lord Jesus, in the vulnerability of our grief we welcome Your beautiful promises—promises of comfort, peace and strength; promises of Your unfailing love and faithful presence. For those living today in a season of especially deep sadness, we ask You to wrap Your arms around them and draw them to Your heart. We're thankful that You are close to the brokenhearted and to those whose spirits have been crushed. We trust You will provide a large measure of Your comfort as we wade through our deep grief. We pray in the name of Jesus, our perfect Comforter. Amen.

GOING DEEPER—GETTING PERSONAL

1. What are some specific things you grieve for your child in regard to his or her mental health challenges?

2. What are some specific things you grieve for *yourself* in regard to your child's challenges?

3. What are some ways you've experienced the Lord's comfort in these areas of grief?

CHAPTER FIVE

The Compassion of Jesus: Living Reflections of His Heart

A GLIMPSE INSIDE

After my previous book, *Unlocking the Treasure*,[1] was published, I would occasionally receive an email from a struggling mom telling me how this study impacted her life. I'll never forget one email I received. This mom gave me a snapshot of the lives of the women within the small gathering she participated in. It was a group of neighborhood moms who had children with a variety of special needs, ranging from physical and cognitive disorders to some very significant mental health issues. Here is an unforgettable excerpt she shared about one of the moms:*

> Another mom is, in her own words, "living in a prison." She and her husband adopted several children from different countries. Each child is struggling with attachment issues and all have psychiatric complications. The story of one of her daughters is especially

---

* Minor details have been changed to protect identities.

tragic. This little girl was serially sexually abused until the age of three. She witnessed members of her family being slaughtered. In a deviant way she had to participate in the "clean up" of other murders. She is damaged beyond words and is acting out in horrific ways. My neighbor cannot even go to the bathroom in her own home without first separating this child from the other children.

The email went on to share some specific, graphic details of what this precious little child endured in her formative years and what her family now grapples with each day. Their reality is beyond our imagination.

When we read stories like this, we can't help but wonder why God allows these things to happen. Our hearts ache when we watch our own child struggle with the effects of a mental illness or a personality disorder. There are times we find ourselves begging God to show some compassion to us and to our children. Maybe there are even times we accuse Jesus of not caring.

It turns out we're not alone in such accusations. The insinuation of "not caring" echoes the sentiments of Jesus' very own disciples and closest friends. In the Gospel of Mark we read that one evening, after a busy day of teaching and healing, Jesus and His disciples settled into a boat and set sail across the Sea of Galilee. A severe storm came up, but Jesus, exhausted from the demands of the day, was sound asleep at the back of the boat. As the storm raged, Jesus seemed oblivious to the sheets of rain lashing down, the high waves breaking onto the boat and the bolts of lightning and booms of thunder tossing their little ship. His disciples finally yelled at Him to wake up! "Teacher, *don't you care* that we're going to drown?"[2]

In Luke we read of how Martha, one of Jesus' dearest friends, eagerly set about throwing a big dinner party for Jesus and His disciples. She felt it very unfair that her sister, Mary, planted herself at Jesus feet, listening to Him teach instead of helping her in the kitchen. "Lord, *don't you care* that my sister has left me to do the work by myself? Tell her to help me!"[3]

In John's Gospel account, we're told that when Martha and Mary's brother, Lazarus, died, they were inconsolably devastated. They had called for Jesus to come. They believed in His power and knew He could heal their dear brother. But Jesus was silent. He didn't come until it was seemingly too late. He didn't go to Martha and Mary until Lazarus had been dead for four days. When they realized Jesus was finally on His way, both women ran out to meet Him with identical words. "Lord, *if only you had been here*, my brother would not have died."[4]

These Gospel stories give voice to the disillusion and confusion those of us who love Jesus sometimes struggle with. When Jesus walked on earth, His closest friends and followers worked side by side with Him. Every day they witnessed His tender care and compassionate heart toward those who suffered. They observed and even participated in His miracles. Yet now, when *they* needed Him so desperately, He seemed silent. Asleep. Absent. Uncaring.

All through the Gospels we read about the gentle, tender compassion of Jesus. So when life gets out of whack in our homes, we find ourselves wondering where the warm-hearted compassion of Jesus is for our children. Our kids have been given heavy burdens to shoulder. Mental illness is painful and debilitating, misunderstood and destructive.

And we parents have a front-row seat. We're often the ones left to pick up the pieces. We cry out to Jesus and sometimes wonder if He just doesn't care. Where is His compassion for us? For our children?

I clearly remember one night following a horrible episode with our son. I collapsed in my chair and tried to release it all to God. I have to admit I released a fair amount of my own anger in the process. I was sick of dealing with my son's behaviors, completely frustrated that we were getting absolutely nowhere with his meds, his therapy, etc. So I had my own little rant with God. "Why won't You help us? Don't You care? Kyle didn't ask for this illness—why won't You show him Your compassion?"

After the steam dissipated a bit, I clearly sensed His Spirit whisper these words of truth to my spirit: "I do care. I show My compassion in many ways. One of the ways I show My compassion to Kyle is through you—through your actions. Those who love and follow Me are My hands and feet in this world. I very intentionally made you Kyle's mom, and you are to show him My love and care. I made YOU to show My compassion to Kyle."

Wow. That wasn't what I expected to hear after my pity party! But those words of truth made me look at things differently. God does manifest His compassion in many ways, and one profound way He shows love to others is to use us as the vessel—the one pouring out His love. We are the body of Christ on earth. We are made in the image of God. *He entrusted His likeness to us!* He created us to reflect His character, to be living expressions of His heart. Can we even begin to grasp what a high calling this is? In regard to our children, no matter their age or diagnosis, God calls us to step into the tenderhearted compassion of Jesus—to clothe ourselves with His kindness, tenderness and grace. We are called to be the very compassion of Jesus to our children.

For those whose child is still living in their home, this calling can be immensely challenging. Indeed, within our own homes is often the most difficult place to serve. Yet, as Priscilla Shirer wrote,

"Wherever you are now is where you are meant to serve now...Your greatest impact will be done here—in the ordinary rhythms of your daily living."[5] We can have an untold impact sharing the compassion of Jesus right here—right in the most ordinary places of life.

Mother Teresa gently said it this way, "Spread love everywhere you go: first of all in your own home. Give love to your children, to your wife or husband...Let no one ever come to you without leaving better and happier. Be the living expression of God's kindness; kindness in your face, kindness in your eyes, kindness in your smile, kindness in your warm greeting."[6]

Be the living expression of God's kindness.

We probably won't receive much accolade or acclaim for being the "living expression of God's kindness" to our raging child. It's more likely that no one will ever know how often we're called to show such difficult compassion, since most don't understand the chaotic dynamics frequently found within our homes. Yet God sees—and He continues to call us to love even our most demanding child with His gentle compassion. Thankfully, He stands ready to help us each step of the way.

So how do we do this? What does it look like to be the compassion of Jesus to our children?

Dan and Rebecca show the compassion and kindness of Jesus in simple, life-giving ways. Their young adult son, Tyler, still lives with them, since he's been unable to launch into adulthood on his own. He struggles with anxiety and a severe mood disorder and is often angry and hostile. Much of the day he keeps to himself, but from time to time he goes off on rants and tirades about how Dan and Rebecca have "ruined his life." Concerned family and friends want Dan and Rebecca to move Tyler out of their home, but they've been unable to find a place for him to live—and they're not willing to let him become a statistic living on the streets. They've decided that for now, being the hands and feet of Jesus to their son means they will provide a safe home for him and help meet his basic needs.

Joan and David Becker[7] beautifully exemplify the compassion of Jesus. Their adult son, Mark, who has a diagnosis of paranoid schizophrenia, is serving a life sentence in prison for the murder of a beloved high school teacher and coach. Joan and David regularly visit Mark in prison, doing their best to make sure his needs are met. More than that, they remind him of their love for him—and the love Jesus has for him. Joan and David encourage Mark to continue to use his gifts and talents in prison, and they maintain regular contact with him through handwritten letters and emails.

Russ and Leslie not only serve as foster parents, but they have also adopted several children with a variety of needs. Each child was severely neglected and abused in their formative years. Though Russ and Leslie have ongoing struggles and challenges with their children, they compassionately love and care for them.

There are an infinite number of ways to show and be the compassion of Jesus to our children. Perhaps it's showing a sincere interest in their off-the-wall hobbies or unique friends. Maybe it's simply calling or texting your child occasionally, working to keep the lines of communication open. Perhaps it's walking away, refusing to respond to the anger stirring inside you when your child is ranting and yelling. Sometimes you're called to display the compassion of Jesus by showing tough love to your child—by calling the police when needed, perhaps allowing your child to spend time in jail, or by making the difficult decision to put your child in a residential home or treatment facility.

Whether our children are living in our home or living far away from home, we can show them the compassion of Jesus through our unwavering love, our provisions, our commitment, our patience and our prayers. We can be the living expression of God's kindness in whatever ways He's asking of us.

Jesus' life is a study in how to treat others with compassion. He demonstrated vast amounts of patience, enjoyed spending quality time with "sinners," treated all people with respect, reached out to rich and ragged alike and was deeply moved by the suffering of others. Jesus was especially drawn to the outcasts of society—the leprous, the shunned, the judged and the unlovable.

And He asks us to do the same.

Jesus looks intently at us and challenges us with the same direct words He spoke to Peter: *"Do you love me? Then take care of my sheep."*[8] Matthew 25:31-46 clearly shows us how to do this. Jesus tells us we are to feed the hungry and thirsty, clothe the naked, take care of the sick and visit those in prison. For many of us reading this book, we don't have to drive to the nearest inner city to be the compassion of Jesus—our very own children are the shunned, the imprisoned, the outcast and the unlovable.

If you're still wondering where the compassion of Jesus is for your child, look in the mirror! *You* have the opportunity to live out His compassion in very tangible ways. *You* have been equipped to be His hands and feet.

"Christ has no body now on earth but yours; no hands but yours; no feet but yours. Yours are the eyes through which the compassion of Christ must look out on the world."[9]

GAZING UP

It's seldom easy being "Jesus with skin on," but we are His body here on earth. 1 John 4:12 declares it plainly: *"No one has ever seen*

God. But if we love each other, God lives in us, and his love is brought to full expression in us" (NLT). We represent—we express—Jesus in this world. And it begins in our homes.

This all sounds good and right and true—and it is—but we're exhausted. Our frazzled hearts achingly cry out, "But who takes care of *us*? How do *we* go on when we're worn out and spent?"

How does Jesus show His compassion to us? After all, it's no small thing being the hands and feet of Jesus, and most of us are weary. Our hearts and emotions are often drained. Does God care? Does God notice when our hearts break for our children? Does it move Him when we sacrifice our money, our time, our energy— *ourselves*—for our kids?

Be assured. God notices and He cares. Deeply. His heart is tender and warm.

Richard Foster, in his book *Prayer: Finding the Heart's True Home*, wrote, "Our God is not made of stone. His heart is the most tender of all. No act goes unnoticed, no matter how insignificant or small. A cup of cold water is enough to put tears in the eyes of God."[10]

Our Father's heart is a heart of compassion—a heart He wants beating in our own chest. And in order for us to love our children well, He first lavishes His love on us. It would be impossible to be the hands and feet of Jesus if we weren't first on the receiving end of His love and compassion. He expresses His all-encompassing love to us in inexhaustible ways.

The parents interviewed feel the heartbeat of Jesus and experience His compassion in a variety of ways throughout their day. They recognize God's care for them through the love, support and provision of those He's placed in their lives. They read His compassionate Words of love in Scripture and hear His tender heart in the gentle whisper of the Holy Spirit. They notice how He extends kindness to them in daily circumstances and experiences. They perceive the grace that flows from the hand of God and refreshes their weary hearts.

Vanessa and Rory readily acknowledge that precisely because of the challenges with their daughter, Sierra, their relationship with Christ is much stronger than when life was smooth sailing. "There are many ways we are different now than we were before all our struggles with Sierra began. Our faith has been put to the test, and God has provided for us in amazing ways. One way we see His compassion and provision is by how He's put others in our lives to help us and walk with us."

Marcy sometimes struggles with knowing how to "speak the truth in love" to her troubled child, as well as to her other children. "I'm thankful, though, that the Spirit gives me wisdom and words in the specific situations we encounter. The Holy Spirit gives me patience and strength. In so many creative ways He encourages me throughout my day."

Ella, too, knows God's compassion is real. "Time and again, we've seen God answer prayers. He was very close to us when our son was in prison and has helped us navigate some very rough years. When we moved to a new community, I was scared and lonely, but God ministered to me in such a way that I realized, perhaps for the first time, how profoundly He loves me. Over the years, God has blessed us with incredible peace."

Kimberly honestly stated, "God has carried me in the past, and He is carrying me through each and every day. There is no way I could have shouldered this heavy burden by myself. Only by the grace of God did I survive those awful years when my daughter was still in our home, wreaking havoc. And it's still only by the strong arms of God that I am able to get through each day, knowing my daughter continues to make such destructive choices. Yes, God's compassion is very real."

Because of His compassionate heart, God notices when we pour out our lives for our children, when we love the unlovable and care for those who are unable to reciprocate our love. He sees our tears and broken hearts, and His heart melts. Our tears are precious to our Heavenly Father, and they move Him to show compassion and comfort. *"God...is the source of all comfort. He comforts us in all our troubles so that we can comfort others. When they are troubled, we will be able to give them the same comfort God has given us"* (2 Cor. 1:3b-4, NLT).

When God proclaimed His name to Moses, we see His compassion, grace, understanding, love and faithfulness all melded into One Holy Name. *"The LORD, the LORD, the compassionate and gracious God, slow to anger, abounding in love and faithfulness"* (Ex. 34:6, NIV).

Jesus is our tenderhearted Shepherd, showing compassion to us and enabling us to show compassion to our children. *"He will feed his flock like a shepherd. He will carry the lambs in his arms, holding them close to his heart. He will gently lead the mother sheep with their young"* (Is. 40:11, NLT).

Additional Scripture to meditate on

Therefore, as God's chosen people, holy and dearly loved, clothe yourselves with compassion, kindness, humility, gentleness and patience....And over all these virtues put on love, which binds them all together in perfect unity. (Col. 3:12, 14, NIV)

What I'm interested in seeing you do is:
sharing your food with the hungry,

inviting the homeless poor into your homes,
  putting clothes on the shivering ill-clad,
  being available to your own families.
Do this and the lights will turn on,
  and your lives will turn around at once.
Your righteousness will pave your way.
  The GOD of glory will secure your passage.
Then when you pray, GOD will answer.
  You'll call out for help and I'll say, "Here I am."

If you get rid of unfair practices,
  quit blaming victims,
  quit gossiping about other people's sins,
If you are generous with the hungry
  and start giving yourselves to the down-and-out,
Your lives will begin to glow in the darkness,
  your shadowed lives will be bathed in sunlight.
I will always show you where to go.
  I'll give you a full life in the emptiest of places —
  firm muscles, strong bones.
You'll be like a well-watered garden,
  a gurgling spring that never runs dry.
(Isaiah 58:7-11, MSG)

*You must be compassionate, just as your Father is
compassionate. (Luke 6:36, NLT)*

*The Lord is good to everyone. He showers compassion on all his
creation. (Psalm 145:9, NLT)*

A prayer to receive the compassion of Jesus

Gentle Shepherd, You love us and our children so deeply and compassionately. May we never lose sight of that truth. Many of our children have suffered in horrific ways, and our minds can't begin to comprehend the abuses some have endured. When our children struggle with the ravages of mental and emotional disorders, our hearts ache with compassion for them.

Thank You for allowing us to come to You with our questions, concerns and even our doubts. We know there are things we will never be able to fully comprehend this side of heaven, but may we never doubt Your love for our children or for us. May we trust You enough to relax in Your enfolding arms of compassion. You loved our children so very much that You entrusted them to us and to our love. May we love them well, Lord. Pour Your Living Water into us, so that we will be able to pour Your love and compassion into the lives of our children. In the name of Jesus, we pray. Amen.

GOING DEEPER—GETTING PERSONAL

1. Do you ever doubt God's love and compassion for your child? For yourself? What brings about those doubts?

2. Mother Teresa exhorted us to be the "living expression of God's kindness." List some ways you have been—and can be—this *living expression of kindness* to your child.

3. How have you been on the receiving end of God's love and compassion? Can you identify some specific ways He's cared for you, especially as you've cared for your child?

CHAPTER SIX

Wildflowers: Treasures of Great Value and Worth

A GLIMPSE INSIDE

"I have often wondered about the wildflowers," contemplated Much-Afraid. "It does seem strange that such unnumbered multitudes should bloom in the wild places of the earth where perhaps nobody ever sees them…"

The look the Shepherd turned on her was very beautiful. "Nothing my Father and I have made is ever wasted," He said quietly, "and the little wildflowers have a wonderful lesson to teach…"[1]

"Nothing my Father and I have made is ever wasted," said the Shepherd.

Patty quietly shared her broken heart, tears flowing down her cheeks. "Chase had so much going for him; his life seemed so promising. He was such a good kid. He excelled at music and was an excellent student. He was truly gifted in so many areas. Then in his late teens, this promising life was completely altered. After he had his first manic-depressive episode and was eventually given the diagnosis of bipolar disorder, it was obvious his life was going to play out much differently than any of us imagined. Chase now has a very hard time focusing on even the simplest of tasks. I grieve all he's lost—his ability to function at the level he once did, his career choices, his relationships. It all seems like such a waste. It just breaks my heart."

Dan and Rebecca, too, often battle that same sense of helplessness for their son, Tyler. Tyler not only struggles with severe mental illness and pervasive developmental disorder, but also with learning disabilities. There are times they wonder what his purpose in life is. Rebecca confided, "I really do believe the message of Jeremiah 29:11[2] and love those verses. I do believe God has a plan and a purpose for every life. So I feel bad when I have a hard time believing it for my own son. I wish I could more clearly see God's purpose for Tyler's life. God is opening my eyes, though. Slowly, but surely, God is showing me His heart of love for Tyler. God loves and values Tyler simply because He made him."

In this very public world of Facebook and Instagram, it's tempting to compare our children's lives and accomplishments (or lack thereof) with those of their peers. Kendra candidly shared how hard it is for her to see updates from high school classmates and read about all the glowing accomplishments of their children. "My friends' kids are pursuing careers, getting married and having babies. I long for my son, Cameron, to experience the same things. Because of his poor mental and emotional health, however, he's been unable to stick it out in college. Thankfully he has a job, but it's a very menial one and he hates it. Cam also struggles in relationships. He would love to have a girlfriend—or even a guy friend to hang around with—but he's been unsuccessful in maintaining long-term friendships of any kind. My son is lonely and unhappy. I truly cannot remember a time Cam was ever happy. To be honest, sometimes I look at Cameron and wonder, what *is* the purpose for his life? Where is the good and perfect plan for Cam?"

These are great questions—questions that probe deeply. Many parents whose children struggle with deep emotional brokenness wonder the same thing.

Society tends to determine the value of others based on achievements, accomplishments, appearances, degrees and even the number of Facebook friends one might have. As parents, we may find ourselves making similar judgments. Perhaps, as we silently wonder about the *purpose* of our child's life, we also find ourselves subconsciously wondering about their *value*. We're very aware that our child isn't contributing to society in ways deemed "successful" by the world's standards. Does this mean, therefore, that their lives are of less value?

My son didn't go to college and hasn't been able to hold down even the most basic of jobs; my friend's son is a doctor. Is her child's life more valuable than my child's? My son has not been successful at maintaining friendships and relationships; most of his high school classmates are married and beginning families. Does this make them more valuable than him?

The first definition that pops up on dictionary.com for the word "value," is "relative worth, merit, or importance." That begs the question, "relative" to what? A further definition of value seems to answer that question: "The worth of something in terms of the amount of other things for which it can be exchanged." Taking this definition to Scripture, we see that Jesus determined our value was worth exchanging His very life for. Jesus willingly gave up His life for mine…His life for yours…His life for your child's life. Jesus sees *each* life as having more worth and value than His very own, whether that life seems to have *purpose* or not.

We are worth everything to Jesus. And so are our children.

Rick Warren's famous book, *The Purpose Driven Life,* emphatically states that Purpose Number One is, "You were planned for God's pleasure." Warren goes on to say, "The moment you were born into the world, God was there as an unseen witness, smiling at your birth. He wanted you alive, and your arrival gave him great pleasure. God did not need to create you, but he chose to create you for his very own enjoyment. You exist for his benefit, his glory, his purpose, his delight…It proves your worth."[3]

Substitute your child's name in place of the word "you," and you will receive the answer to your child's worth, value and purpose. Powerful, isn't it? Maybe you need to reread this several times and allow the fullness of God's delight to fill your heart. God delights in your child. He is crazy about our children and is not put off by their emotional illnesses.

Our children have immeasurable worth and value because they are known intimately by their Creator. He fashioned and made them just as He planned. He did not make a mistake when He *"knit them together in the secret place."*[4] He loves them fully and completely, whether they are successfully earning more money than they can spend or they're living off government funding and whatever other money they can scrape together.

Our child's purpose in life may look very different than the dreams we had for them when they were little. Our children may never be well-known by the masses or rise to stardom as they make their mark in this world. As Much-Afraid contemplated, "It does seem strange that such unnumbered multitudes should bloom in the wild places of the earth where perhaps nobody ever sees them." Yes, perhaps no one sees our children and they live "invisible" lives. This does not mean, however, that their lives are empty or void of purpose and value. They are seen and loved by their Creator, and as the Shepherd told Much-Afraid, "They have a wonderful lesson to teach."

Our children, too, have wonderful lessons to teach. Many of our kids are the bravest, strongest, most resilient people we could meet. Patty admires how her son Chase works hard to stay on top of his mental health. "He is very proactive in taking care of himself. He exercises, eats well, sees his doctor and therapist regularly, and has even checked himself into treatment when he knew he was relapsing." Chase is very aware that his mental illness has changed his life in huge ways. He daily combats brain fog, weariness and confusion. He struggles with loneliness and anxiety. Yet instead of wallowing in self-pity that his life is following such a difficult path, he is rising above it and living each day as best as possible. Who's to say Chase isn't living out his purpose in life—giving God great pleasure—by simply taking one day at a time, bravely battling the silent storm in his brain?

Many of our children model the qualities of perseverance and endurance, inner strength and fortitude. One psychiatrist told my husband and me that the energy and emotion Kyle exerts to simply get through each day takes more of a toll on him than we can imagine. Most of us don't know what it takes to live and function with such anxiety or what it's like to live out of sync with those around us. But our children do. Their struggles are real. We would do well to watch and learn from our children as they experience life on such a difficult playing field.

God uses our children not only as models to watch and learn from, but as instruments of change. After talking with and listening to many parents, it is obvious God uses our children and the challenges they bring to change our hearts—and often the hearts of other members of our family—molding us ever closer to the image of Christ. Because of our children, we've spent time on the other side of unconditional love—discovering we are able to love even those who cannot or will not reciprocate our love. We have learned how to remain calm and patient as we've parented angry, raging children. We've learned difficult lessons of surrender, relinquishment and trust, being called to release our children in ways we never dreamed. We have learned how to advocate for our children and how to stand up and speak for those who have no voice. We've learned we are stronger than we thought, able to persist and endure in even the harshest of circumstances. We've learned how to look outside the box, to see life through a different lens. We have learned valuable lessons in sacrifice as we've been called to surrender untold amounts of finances, energy, emotion, time and prayer. We have learned to delight in simple pleasures, finding flashes of joy, beauty and hope in small achievements.

Yes, each of our children's purpose in life might play out in very different ways than we ever anticipated. But that does not mean their lives are without purpose and meaning—or of less value than others'. God has a beautiful message of grace for each one of us: "God loves you unconditionally just as you are, and not as you should be, because no one is ever as they should be."[5] God loves your child with that same unconditional, unrestricted love.

"God saw ALL that He had made, and it was very good" (Gen. 1:31, NIV).

GAZING UP

Jesus told His disciples, *"Look at the birds. They don't plant or harvest or store food in barns, for your Heavenly Father feeds them. And aren't you far more valuable to Him than they are?...Look at the lilies of the field and how they grow....If God cares so wonderfully for the wildflowers that are here today and thrown into the fire tomorrow, he will certainly care for you" (Matt. 6:26, 28, 30, NLT).*

What a beautiful description of God's love for us. He loves us simply because He made us. He loves us—not because of who we are or what we can do for Him—but because of who HE is and because of what HE has done for us. God loves and values each life He's created.

From the dawn of time, it was God's decision to create people to live in relationship with Him. Using His skillful, gentle hands, He molded the first living being from the dust of the ground—shaping this being with perfect precision until he satisfied the eye of the Creator. To give this being life, He breathed His own Spirit-breath into him. God then crowned the highlight of His creation with His blessing. When finished, He proclaimed His creation *very good!* [6]

God continues to fashion and create each and every life. When He chose to make our children, He flawlessly formed and fashioned them in His image—after His own likeness. Each of our children, regardless of ability, has the potential to reflect God's glory. Our children are deeply valued and adored by their Creator.

King David wrote a beautiful, poetic rendition of what happens in the womb before a baby sees the light of day. Listen to the lyrical words of Psalm 139:13-18 (NIV).

For you created my inmost being;
  you knit me together in my mother's womb.
I praise you because I am fearfully and wonderfully made;
  your works are wonderful,
  I know that full well.
My frame was not hidden from you

when I was made in the secret place,
when I was woven together in the depths of the earth.
Your eyes saw my unformed body;
 all the days ordained for me were written in your book
 before one of them came to be.
How precious to me are your thoughts, God!
 How vast is the sum of them!
Were I to count them,
 they would outnumber the grains of sand—
 when I awake, I am still with you.

Just as you did with the previous Rick Warren quote, read these verses out loud and insert your child's name in place of the personal pronouns. This will give you a vivid reminder that your child is first and foremost HIS child—and that he or she, too, bears the beautiful image of the Creator. Your child does indeed have immense value!

The Good Shepherd values all life and longs for none to be wasted. While it is possible for people to waste their lives and squander the gifts He's given, God's intention and plan for each life is to blossom into all He's desired for us and all He's created us to be. As parents of children who have such difficulty functioning in this world, we grieve for what could have been and we grieve for what is. But let's not be too quick to see their lives as a waste or to think for a moment they are not valued by their Creator. It's very important for us to remember that God's heart for His children (including that very difficult child He placed within your home) is one of love, patience and understanding. God created your child. He sees your child's heart and understands his/her brokenness. Please, don't misunderstand. God does not turn a blind eye to their sin or pat them on the head and give them a free pass to do whatever their impulses demand, but it's important we let God be God. He understands our child's illness and brokenness on a level we will never comprehend.

We can rest in the awareness that God understands and loves our children more than we possibly could. God knows what drives our children and what has damaged their minds and emotions. When our children act out in harmful, destructive ways, and possibly face some serious consequences, it's easy to become discouraged by the chaos. When our children make catastrophic choices, perhaps we look at their lives and wonder why a loving God allowed this to happen. Though we grieve over the damage they have caused, we still deeply love them and hold them in our hearts as our precious children.

When we wonder if *God* still loves them and still sees their worth, when we find ourselves deep in the valley and questioning God's love, we need to look up. Way up. Over the mountains and to the cross.

In his powerful book, *Moving Mountains*, John Eldredge wrote these compelling words: "Oh, how it helps me to remind myself, I am praying to the One who gave his life for me. When we look to the stormy seas of our circumstances to try and assure ourselves God is loving, we are fighting a losing battle. That is why we have to go to the true 'fixed point' in the universe—the man hanging in execution on Calvary's hilltop."[7]

God, in His sacrificial love, has a perfect understanding of our children. In Psalm 103:14, David wrote, *"For he (God) knows how we are formed, he remembers that we are dust" (NIV).*

God intimately knows the struggles our children face—their brain damage, their illnesses, their wounds and their brokenness. He knows what's behind every angry, shouted word, each rambling thought, each paralyzing bout of anxiety. He saw the abuses they endured. He understands the frustrations they live with. He perceives the fears that plague them. He weeps for our children and promises that someday all will be made right. Someday, this fallen, broken world will be fully redeemed.

While we can't altogether know how God will deal with and adjudicate the harmful (even sinful) choices some of our children have made, we can know this: The heart of Jesus beats with love for our children, and His blood stained the cross for them, too. God is a righteous God, looking at our hearts more than our actions. When He judges everyone on earth, He will be honest and fair.

"For we (and our children) are God's masterpiece. He created us anew in Christ Jesus..." (Eph. 2:10, NLT).

Additional Scripture to meditate on

...You are a people set apart as holy to God, your God. God, your God, chose you out of all the people on Earth for himself as a cherished, personal treasure. (Deut. 7:6, MSG)

...He knows the number of hairs on your head! Never fear, you are far more valuable to him than a whole flock of sparrows. (Luke 12:7, TLB)

For we are God's masterpiece. He has created us anew in Christ Jesus, so we can do the good things he planned for us long ago. (Eph. 2:10, NLT)

A prayer of love

Creator God, there is so much mystery surrounding the creation of our children. We don't understand why some of our children were afflicted with mental illness—why their minds were knit together the way they were. Our hearts struggle, too, with the reality that some of our children were emotionally damaged and forever scarred by the abuses they endured at the cruel hands of others.

Yet we know You created this world perfectly—no blemishes or brokenness. We realize this perfection was suspended when sin entered the world. The fallout of sin has affected us all, including our precious children. We stand on the promise, though, that someday You will restore and redeem Your creation! For now, even as we struggle with our children and their issues, help us know and remember that You see our children as beautiful wildflowers pushing through the cracks and crevices of life. Just as You have bestowed value on the birds of the air and the flowers of the field, so You esteem and value our children. Open our eyes to see the plan and purpose You have for them and continue to use our children to teach and shape us. Thank You for Your boundless love. In Jesus' name we pray. Amen.

GOING DEEPER—GETTING PERSONAL ————

1. Re-read Rick Warren's quote from earlier in the chapter, inserting your child's name in place of the word "you." What emotions does this bring to the surface?

2. In what ways is your child an unseen wildflower? Has he or she ever been overlooked by society? Frowned on as a nuisance? Trampled underfoot by others?

3. How is your child seen by the Creator of the universe? Write out some descriptive words God uses to describe your child from His viewpoint.

4. In the allegory quoted at the beginning of this chapter, the Shepherd, speaking of unseen wildflowers, told Much-Afraid, "They have a wonderful lesson to teach." Can you identify some lessons you or others have learned from your child's life? How has God used your child as an instrument of change?

CHAPTER SEVEN

Making Sense of Suffering: Our Children's—Our Own

Part One*

A GLIMPSE INSIDE

Recently I sent a friend an email asking how things were going for her family. She was very honest in her reply as she told me about their gut-wrenching week with their daughter, who struggles with severe RAD (reactive attachment disorder). She wrote, "I do not enjoy roller coaster rides and find myself screaming to get off. Why does God have us go through times like these—with our kids suffering even more than we are?"

My friend named it well. Suffering. Sometimes, in the midst of rages, obsessions and meltdowns, we don't always recognize or acknowledge the suffering of our children. Yet, when we contemplate things a little more intently, we see it. It breaks our hearts, and we don't understand why God allows it.

---

* Since the topic of suffering is so multifaceted, it is covered in two chapters. Part One constitutes **A Glimpse Inside** and considers the suffering our children endure due to their brain disorders, as well as the suffering parents experience because of their child's mental or emotional illness. Part Two constitutes **Gazing Up** and uses Scripture to more fully delve into the mystery of suffering.

The concept of suffering is a difficult one, especially for a believer. It's an emotionally laden topic, one rife with confusion. We want so badly to be able to make sense of it, but there are times we simply can't. There are few things worse than watching our child suffer and not be able to love them to wholeness; it's truly its own hellish brand of pain. When our children suffer, we suffer.

In this chapter, we will take a close look at the suffering our children endure, as well as the suffering parents experience because of their child's mental or emotional illness. In Chapter 8, we will explore what Scripture teaches about suffering.

Our children and their suffering

Whitney shared the painful story of her daughter's emotional suffering:

> We were surprised to discover we were expecting our fourth child! Our three older children, already in their teens, were less than thrilled. But Dustin and I quickly adjusted to the idea and eagerly anticipated our new little gift from God. Things have turned out so very differently than we ever would have imagined. Peyton has been a difficult child since birth. Even as an infant, we could sense something was wrong. She pushed us away, didn't respond to our cuddles or touch and wouldn't look at us. Peyton was a profoundly unhappy child. Even when she was a toddler we found ourselves walking on eggshells around her. She had incredible meltdowns and rages, and we never knew

what would set her off. We suspected autism. By age three we had begun bringing her to various doctors, as well as a counselor.

Peyton's first hospitalization occurred at age seven. Seven. It was the most heartrending thing we've ever had to do, but she desperately needed help. We knew it was no longer safe to keep her home—not for us, nor for Peyton. We needed to lock our doors with special locks, as well as hide anything dangerous, such as knives, scissors, ball bats, glass objects, etc. We couldn't leave Peyton alone for even a minute, as she often tried to harm herself. Peyton also began running away—not in the amusing, cute way of a more typical seven-year-old, but as a child in the throes of psychosis. It was heartbreaking. She often made comments such as, "I just want to go to heaven. I don't want to be here anymore."

Peyton was in the hospital for two weeks and received a diagnosis of early-onset bipolar disorder and generalized anxiety disorder. It was a painful time for all of us. We knew she needed to be there, but she didn't understand why. After each family therapy session, Peyton would cry and beg to come home with us. She needed a security guard to hold her back so we could leave. After two weeks, Peyton was discharged and spent several more weeks in the partial-hospitalization program.

Things are now going somewhat better, but she will still make the occasional comment about wanting to die and go to heaven. We sense Peyton continues to suffer deep inside.

Suffering. Many of our kids are the bravest people we know. We can hardly imagine the strength and energy they need to simply get through each day. Our children face challenges unknown to most others. Their invisible disorders silently storm within their psyches, causing turmoil, angst and fogginess in the hidden recesses of heart and mind.

Rita shared that her son, Barry, struggled with suicidal ideations for many of his early years. The first time he talked seriously about committing suicide was at age eight. At age eleven, he explained in vivid detail the many ways he could kill himself. It was all he could think about or talk about, and he was finally hospitalized. By age twelve, it was recommended that Barry spend several months in a residential facility. Rita said the long-term treatment was helpful, but because of his severe anxieties, the hospitalizations and residential stay caused Barry to suffer years of recurring nightmares. Barry eventually underwent Electroconvulsive Therapy (ECT) to gain some relief for his treatment-resistant depression and severe anxiety. Though the ECT helped for a time, Barry lost all his childhood memories, and eventually his relentless anxiety returned. Rita said Barry, now in his twenties, lives a very lonely, isolated life. She told me, "I'm so proud of Barry. He's been very sick for fifteen years, but he hasn't given up. He is very kind and compassionate. I wish others could see him for who he is. For me, being a daily observer of his suffering is almost unbearable."

Parents confided the pain of watching their children suffer through relationship failures, job losses, personality changes, abusive relationships, homelessness and imprisonment. Many moms painfully shared how difficult it is to see their young children confused by their inability to make and keep friends. One father told of the anguish of watching his young son go from being a typical, healthy teenager to becoming an irrational, angry young man who was eventually diagnosed with paranoid schizophrenia.

There is a saying that a parent is only as happy as their unhappiest child. Whether we agree with this statement or not, we can all understand the emotions behind it. When we see our children suffering and we're unable to take away their pain, it's as if a knife is being thrust into our own heart. When we explore this thought a little deeper—especially in light of Scripture—we see that this kind of pain and suffering has Satan's fingerprints all over it. Satan takes perverse delight in battering God's children with pain, knowing that what hurts them affects the heart of their loving, compassionate Father. The same principle applies to us. What hurts our children hurts us. When they are suffering, we too are suffering.

Our Suffering

Lana shared her story of pain with me:

> I've never shared this part of our story with anyone. Jadyn was always a very difficult child, and nothing seemed to please her. In addition to being extremely moody, she had severe sensory issues. If I cut her toast the wrong way, or poured her milk into the wrong glass, or peeled her banana incorrectly, she would have a complete meltdown, potentially resulting in a rage that lasted for hours. Finding clothes that felt

"right" was an ongoing nightmare, and words can't begin to express the difficulty of transitioning from one season to the next. But bedtimes were the worst. Jadyn would not stay in her bed or in her room no matter what we tried. We read all the parenting books and got all the advice, but NOTHING worked for long. We lived in a constant state of exhaustion, frustration and discouragement.

As the years progressed, we sought professional help and began to somewhat understand Jadyn's struggles. We dealt with them as best we could but continued to walk on eggshells. None of Jadyn's growing-up years were easy, but she seemed to really bottom out in the latter years of high school. We weren't sure if it was the anxiety of impending college and adulthood, or hormones, or simply her life experiences that led to such upheaval. We continued to try to help her with counseling, etc., but she continued to unravel.

The breaking point for us came when she attacked me. (And this is the part I've never shared with anyone.) One evening when I was working in the kitchen, Jadyn came in and asked for money to buy a pair of shoes. I told her she would need to use her own money to buy them, as they weren't really necessary. She became very upset with me as I tried to reason with her. I realized we weren't getting anywhere, so I told her we'd talk about it later—after she calmed down. As she stormed out of the room she gave me a hard shove. I lost my balance and fell over a kitchen chair, resulting in some broken ribs. I did not tell my doctor how it happened—I guess I had a misguided sense of wanting to protect my daughter. She was eighteen years old at the time, and I didn't want her to get into legal trouble. Looking back, I often wonder if that was the right thing to do. Besides wanting to protect Jadyn legally, I think I was also protecting myself. I felt an enormous sense of shame that my daughter hurt me so deeply (physically and emotionally). I didn't want anyone else to see my private humiliation and suffering.

Indeed, our children do suffer greatly with their mental and emotional illnesses. But make no mistake, our children's severe emotional disorders bring much suffering to us parents, too, as well as to others living in the home.

Parents shared various ways they've suffered because of their child's mental illness or personality disorder.

Helen's adult daughter, Addi, has a diagnosis of antisocial personality disorder. True to form, Addi's life has been characterized by deceitfulness, hostility, aggression and lack of restraint. All throughout Addi's childhood and teen years, Helen struggled with Addi's compulsive lying, her incredibly strong will and her total lack of regard for others. For Helen—physically and emotionally—the toll was great. "I was constantly being pulled into Addi's issues, and it was literally making me sick. For my own health I finally had to move several states away once Addi reached adulthood. Even though a parent is never really finished with a child like Addi, I felt I had done everything I could for her. The time came when I knew I simply needed to get away from her."

Judy told me of her struggle with depression during her son's growing-up years. Darren, who has a diagnosis of autism spectrum disorder, was a very challenging child. "I was often depressed. I constantly felt like a failure at marriage and a failure at parenting."

Our children's mental and emotional illnesses not only cause many parents to suffer with their physical and/or emotional health, it also causes many families to suffer financially.

Whitney, whose story is shared in the opening of this chapter, said the cost of the medications and ongoing counselling for Peyton is overwhelming. "It's been very hard for us to stay on top of things financially. We recently made the decision to downsize our home in order to better afford the care Peyton needs."

Rita, whose young son, Barry, spent many months in a residential care facility and underwent several ECT treatments, can well relate to the emotional, physical and financial suffering parents often endure. "Having a child with a chronic mental illness definitely takes a toll on parents. My husband and I both have struggled with depression. I also deal with Crohn's disease, inflammatory arthritis, diabetes and fibromyalgia. Besides the emotional and physical toll, the financial demand has been overwhelming. We used our retirement savings to help cover the cost of Barry's residential treatment, which was unbelievably expensive. The ECT treatments amounted to several thousand dollars and were not covered by our insurance. Thankfully, many of the doctors involved in Barry's care were willing to drop or reduce their fees, but it was still very costly. We were willing to do anything, though, to get the care he so desperately needed."

Brad and Lucinda shared how they've suffered in various ways because of their daughter, Haley, who has a diagnosis of reactive attachment disorder, antisocial disorder and bipolar disorder. Brad relates, "When Haley was thirteen years old, we just couldn't do it any longer. Her challenges were taking a severe toll on Lucinda physically, and it was negatively affecting our marriage. In addition, we had no energy for our other kids. We decided to send Haley to a Christian therapeutic boarding school during the second half of her eighth-grade year. Even though this school cost a thousand dollars a month (out of pocket), we were willing to pay, as we had few other options at that point. Unfortunately, after being there a year, the staff told us Haley was not receptive to the program and had made no efforts to change. We had no choice but to take her back home. The nightmare continued throughout her teen years, with Haley often running away. She left home for good at age seventeen and is now in her early twenties. We're terribly concerned for her and agonize over the choices she's made, but for the protection of our other children—as well as ourselves—we have very little contact with her. The pain, though, never quite goes away."

Several parents sadly shared that the relationships with their families and others have suffered as a direct result of their child's troubled mental health. Many talked about the "cloud" that seems to hang over their families, causing turmoil and strain. Most all of the parents interviewed said their marriages were affected one way or another. One mom said their different parenting styles, particularly in dealing with their son's rages, made things incredibly stressful between her and her husband. Another told me, "My husband deals with our daughter's issues by becoming very introverted. For example, he will go to bed very early just to get away. This hurts me because I want to talk through the problems we're dealing with." One father shared, "Some of my friends have expressed surprise that my wife and I are still married, considering the stress we live with on a daily basis."

Siblings suffer as well. Having a brother or sister with a mental or emotional disorder can be embarrassing and frustrating. It is not unusual for the other children to deal with the drama in their homes by acting out in difficult ways. One mom shared, "Our two older kids are often embarrassed by their younger sister. They no longer want to have friends over, and I see my oldest daughter becoming more and more withdrawn. Our seventeen-year-old son is beginning to act out as well. He was recently arrested for drunk driving, which is so out of character for him. Because of our youngest daughter's severe issues, she's taking more and more of our time. This is making it increasingly hard to have any one-on-one time with the older two. I see our family unraveling." We will more fully explore the suffering of siblings in Chapter 14.

Parents and siblings spoke of the frustration of trying to enjoy a family vacation or any kind of family outing. Time and again families find their plans hijacked by rages, anxieties and other troublesome behaviors. Connie told me, "The last family vacation we took was when Will was ten. We love to camp and typically would go several times a year. The last time we went, however, Will had a horrible rage. We were in a crowded campground, and I can only imagine what the other campers thought. We never went camping again and eventually sold our camper."

Suffering. Our children's, our own. How do we make sense of it? When our child is in the throes of mental illness, it's almost impossible not to focus on the darkness. We find our very lives organized around the illness, the behaviors, the intense chaos and disorder. When Kyle was in his early twenties, one of the medications he had been on for years became toxic in his system. This necessitated a medication change, and things became almost intolerable as he became increasingly volatile and unstable. One difficult evening I journaled my emotions as I processed the current state of life in our home:

Lord, this season is so hard. Going through this med change is about more than we can take. Kyle is angry, loud and restless. He paces and talks AT us nonstop. There's a new hole in the kitchen wall, and his room is tossed upside down. There are doctor appointments, psychiatry appointments, lab appointments and trips to the pharmacy. All the while, it's the holiday season, so outwardly I'm decorating the Christmas tree and stringing lights and playing Christmas carols—but privately I'm sitting in the dark, crying.

When we're surrounded by the dark chaos of emotional instability and can't catch even a glimmer of light to reveal the end of the tunnel, where do we find hope? A Band-Aid box of religious clichés and spiritual platitudes doesn't suffice when the pain is so profound. Self-help books and philosophical tomes seem to offer more confusion than solutions. So where do we go to help us navigate the dark tunnel of suffering?

In my own journey, I've found there's only one place to find sufficient answers to the age-old questions of pain and suffering. And many of the parents interviewed have discovered the same truth.

As parent after parent shared their painful stories—often with tears streaming down their cheeks—many also shared their deep faith. Faith in the One who tenderly holds them in the darkness. Faith in the One who is able to shed light on the whys of suffering. Faith in the One who always has a purpose and a plan, even within the murky confusion of mental illness.

Faith in the One whose first recorded words shattered the darkness: "Let there be LIGHT."

The fullness of God's plan didn't stop there. God continued His work from creation to the cross. On the day of Jesus' crucifixion, darkness once again covered the earth for a time. Satan, the prince of darkness, must have surely thought he had won the war. But when Jesus' work on the cross was complete, He shattered the darkness once and for all with His inextinguishable light.

And the light of Jesus continues to beam down from the cross to our current crisis. Satan, whose purpose in life is to steal, kill and destroy, knows he lost the ultimate battle. Yet he is still active on earth, using suffering and pain to cloak our lives with darkness, hoping to snuff out the Light of Christ. But the prophetic words recorded in John 1:5 still ring out today with truthful clarity: *"The light shines in the darkness, and the darkness has not overcome it."*

Not even the darkness of mental illness has the power to overcome and extinguish the Light of Christ.

When we're finally able to lift our despondent gaze to Jesus—to shift our focus from the cruel schemes of Satan to the brilliant goodness of God—we will find hope. Jesus looks into our despairing eyes with intense love and gently beckons, *"I am the light of the world. Whoever follows me will never walk in the darkness, but will have the light of life"* (John 8:12).

It is only by walking in His Light that life begins to make sense. Yes, the journey is incredibly painful and scary when our child is battling mental illness. And it's okay to honestly acknowledge our suffering and that of our children. If we cannot get beyond it, though, we will eventually find ourselves stuck in the dark quagmire of our misery. Jesus comes to us right where we are and offers to pull us out of this pit. Can we trust Him? Can we allow Him to help us make sense of our suffering?

In the next chapter, we will delve into some various themes found in Scripture regarding suffering in the life of a believer—and why God allows it.

Additional Scripture to meditate on

For with you is the fountain of life; in your light we see light.
(Psalm 36:9, NIV)

My comfort in my suffering is this:
Your promise preserves my life. (Psalm 119:50, NIV)

Because of the Lord's great love we are not consumed,
for his compassions never fail.
They are new every morning;
great is your faithfulness.
I say to myself, "The Lord is my portion;
therefore I will wait for him."
The Lord is good to those whose hope is in him,
to the one who seeks him… (Lam. 3:22-25, NIV)

Prayer for those in the midst of suffering

Father, in our suffering help us to remember that You give us grace for today, and then tomorrow You will bless us with a whole new supply of Yourself. We receive Your sweet presence each moment, and rest securely in You. Lord, may we keep firmly in mind that even when we don't know what the outcome of our situation will be, it is safe not to know because You are God and You are good. We trust You, Jesus, and pray in Your name. Amen. [1]

GOING DEEPER—GETTING PERSONAL ———————

1. What are some painful ways you've seen your child suffer?

2. How have you suffered as a direct result of your child's brain disorder? How have others in your family suffered? Explore some ways you've struggled emotionally, physically, financially, etc.

3. Do you find it difficult to trust God in the midst of suffering? Why or why not?

CHAPTER EIGHT

Making Sense of Suffering: Our Children's—Our Own

Part Two

In Chapter Seven, we looked at various ways our children suffer as a result of their mental illness and emotional disorders. We also acknowledged how we, as parents, struggle with our own suffering because of our children's issues. In Part Two, we're going to shine the light of Scripture on the darkness of suffering. The theme verse for this book gives us an astounding promise: "*I will give you treasures hidden in the darkness—secret riches. I will do this so you may know that I am the Lord, the God of Israel, the one who calls you by name*" (Isaiah 45:3, NLT).

As we struggle with suffering, familiar, age-old questions encroach into our thinking: *What good could possibly come out of this? Why did God allow this to happen? Does Jesus even see or care? Is God really good?*

As we wrestle intensely with these questions, it's only fair that we bring them to God. He's likely the One with whom we're upset, whether we admit that or not. We know God is sovereign and all-powerful, and we innately know He's the One who could fix things and make them better. So when God doesn't work as we had hoped He would, our response is often to blame God and accuse Him of not caring. Christian author Stormy O'Martian, however, makes a very good point for us to consider: "Often people blame God for the tragedies in their lives and close themselves off from the very One who can take their pain away. But we won't make that same mistake if we will remember two things: 1) God is good; and 2) Satan comes to steal, kill and destroy. It's crucial not to confuse the two during a time of loss."[1] For our reading, let's paraphrase the last sentence: *It's crucial not to confuse the two during a time of suffering.*

God is good. Satan comes to steal, kill and destroy. With these words echoing through our minds, let's see what Scripture says about suffering.

GAZING UP

> *God, you're my last chance of the day. I spend the night on my knees before you. I call to you, God; all day I call. I wring my hands, I plead for help. Does your love make any difference? Why, God, do you turn a deaf ear? Why do you make yourself scarce? For as long as I remember I've been hurting; I've taken the worst you can hand out, and I've had it. I'm bleeding, black-and-blue. The only friend I have left is Darkness.*

Raw emotions. Passionate, critical words flung at the Almighty from someone in deep emotional pain. Indeed, this diatribe was penned by a man who had hit the bottom in his suffering. I'm not sure what was causing his pain or what his precise struggles were, but he's completely transparent in his frustration and disillusionment with God.

How do *you* handle your suffering? Do you dare speak to God like this man did? Do you think God is okay with us being that honest? Actually, He is. In fact, these words were taken directly from Psalm 88.[2] This unique Psalm gives the reader no pat answers, nor even the tiniest glimmer of hope. The Psalmist is painfully vulnerable in his emotions as he expresses his heart to God.

When we look at suffering in the light of Scripture, we discover it's a topic that's well-covered. God has much to say about suffering, and He has many sacred promises that cover every aspect of it. In addition to Scripture, countless books have been written that also deal with suffering. It's a topic that's been explored and questioned and wrestled with since the days of Job. And with good reason. *We all suffer.* There is not a person in this world who has not experienced suffering. It's part of our fallen, human condition.

The secular world insists that personal comfort, freedom, acquisition and happiness are to be our highest goals and that we should eschew suffering at all costs. But that is not Scripture's narrative. The message of Scripture allows much room for suffering. In fact, suffering is at the very heart of the Christian story.

And it all points to Christ.

Scripture tells us Jesus took not only our sin, but also our suffering with Him to the cross. He willingly endured it because He knew it would be for our redemption. He experienced our suffering on the cross, and He experiences it with us today. There's not an emotional burden we or our children carry that Christ is not carrying with us.

When we are deep in despair, like the anguished author of Psalm 88, there's only one place—one Person—who offers the hope our desperate hearts long for. His name is Jesus. Timothy Keller, in his excellent book *Walking with God through Pain and Suffering* wrote, "Suffering is unbearable if you aren't certain that God is for you and with you."[3] How true that is. The lives we live, and the struggles we watch our children endure, would be intolerable if we were not certain God has a plan and a purpose for the suffering and that He is walking with us each step of the way.

With this in mind, let's explore a few key points Scripture makes about suffering, as well as the promises of HOPE that go hand in hand with them.

When we examine our lives through the lens of Scripture, the first thing that becomes clear is that we *shouldn't be surprised* at our suffering or at the suffering of our children. Jesus told us it would be like this. In John 16:33, Jesus, speaking to His disciples, plainly stated, *"I have told you these things, so that in me you may have peace. In this world you WILL have trouble. But take heart! I have overcome the world"* (emphasis added).

Other translations use the word, "tribulation," in place of "trouble." *Strong's Greek Dictionary of the New Testament*[4] clarifies the word "tribulation" by offering these synonyms: affliction, anguish, burden, persecution, suffering, trouble. The definition also speaks of crushing; compressing; squeezing; a heavy, burdensome weight; and agitation.

Do any of these sound familiar?

We do not yet live in a perfected world. We live in a world where Satan has a lot of freedom to stalk and roam, hunting for prey. In fact, 1 Peter 5:8 tells us the devil *"prowls around like a roaring lion looking for someone to devour."* Until Jesus returns and ushers in a flawless new paradise, suffering will be a reality in our lives.

Another point Scripture makes about suffering is that there is always a *purpose* for it. God uses suffering to refine and mature our faith. The apostle Peter, who suffered in unimaginable ways, penned these words: *"There is wonderful joy ahead, even though you must endure many trials for a little while. These trials will show that your faith is genuine. It is being tested as fire tests and purifies gold— though your faith is far more precious than mere gold. So when your faith remains strong through many trials, it will bring you much praise and glory and honor on the day when Jesus Christ is revealed to the whole world"* (1 Peter 1:6b-7, NLT).

The apostle James chimed in with these powerful words: *"Consider it pure joy, my brothers and sisters, whenever you face trials of many kinds, because you know that the testing of your faith produces perseverance. Let perseverance finish its work so that you may be mature and complete, not lacking anything"* (James 1:2-4).

When we are in relationship with Christ, God uses suffering not only to refine and mature us, but also as a means of drawing us closer to Him. Keller wrote, "Suffering can strengthen our relationship to God as nothing else can. C.S. Lewis's famous dictum is true, that in prosperity God whispers to us, but in adversity he shouts to us. Suffering is indeed a test of our connection to God."[5]

Kent and Steph agree with this wholeheartedly. They know their connection to God has been strengthened because of the struggles they have with their daughter, Lainie. They also acknowledge that, as a side benefit, they once again find themselves praying together. "We haven't done that since the early days of our marriage. As life got busy, our prayer times together dropped off. We've rediscovered the beauty of praying together. Our challenges with Lainie have drawn us closer to God and closer to each other."

Scripture also urges us to be *patient* in our suffering. The apostle James reminds his fellow-sufferers to *persevere*, following the example of Job.[6] Indeed, many of the parents I spoke with seem to have the patience of Job! Ron and Jo Ellen have four children with mental health issues, as well as challenges with their own mental health. Daily, they live with hassles, heartaches and upheavals few of us could imagine. They credit God for giving them the strength and perseverance they need to get through each day.

Another comforting point Scripture makes about suffering is that we are *never alone or forgotten* in our pain. Never. No matter how alone or abandoned we might feel, we can count on God's comforting promise found in Psalm 23:4. *"Even when I walk through the darkest valley, I will not be afraid, for you are close beside me"* (NLT). Hebrews 13:5 is another much-loved passage that gives us great assurance. *"God has said, 'Never will I leave you; never will I forsake you.'"*

This promise is a great comfort to Victoria, whose husband, unable to cope with the stresses of life, left her after thirty years of marriage. She knows that even though her husband chose to leave, God never will. "My relationship with God is very strong, very close. He has blessed me with deep faith and much trust. I honestly don't worry about things like finances. I don't worry about falling apart, even when things are really rough with my kids. I know God is walking right alongside me."

Scripture also reminds us to maintain an *eternal perspective* on suffering. Romans 8:18 promises that *"what we suffer now is nothing compared to the glory he (God) will reveal to us later."* On some dark days, I find myself flipping straight through the pages of Scripture to read the end of the Book, reminding myself of the rest of the story! Revelation 21 and 22 speak of the absolute purity, glory and perfection that awaits us on the new earth. This old earth, with all its brokenness and pain, will not last forever. Someday, we will hear a shout emanating from the throne room of heaven. *"Look, God's home is now among his people! He will wipe every tear from their eyes, and there will be no more death or sorrow or crying or pain. All these things are gone forever!"* (Rev. 21:3-4, NLT).

In the here and now, though, we're given permission to unload our suffering, struggles, and anger onto God. Emulating the author of Psalm 88, we can freely pour out our heart to the Lord with all the honesty we can muster. He is patient and gentle with us. He understands our confusion and grief. He wants us to come to Him with our suffering. His shoulders are broad and strong.

Rita experienced a season of deep anger at God when her son's incapacitating anxiety prevented him from completing college. Rita told me, "When I confessed to a friend how angry I was, she assured me it was okay. She reminded me that God can certainly handle my anger!"

Whitney shared, "This is not the script I had written for Peyton's life, and for a while I was very angry that God didn't follow my script. But as time went by, God gave me peace about living out *His* plan for our lives."

Another point about suffering that Scripture makes clear is that we, as followers of Christ, are called to *share in the suffering* of Jesus. The apostle Paul spelled out his longing to intimately know Christ. He wrote, *"I want to know Christ—yes, to know the power of his resurrection and participation in his sufferings, becoming like him in his death." (Phil 3:10, NIV)*. Part of knowing Christ intimately—and being conformed into His image—is to share in His suffering. What trials and suffering did Jesus endure, beside His horrific crucifixion? The Bible study *Unlocking the Treasure*[7] considered several ways Jesus suffered while here on earth—and how we can share in His suffering:

- People rejected Him, even though He loved and cared for everyone. *Jesus understands when we experience rejection from the people closest to us.*
- Jesus had to deal with being misunderstood, even by His most devoted disciples. *Jesus knows what we're going through when we*

feel misunderstood and judged by other parents, family members, school teachers and church members.

- Jesus suffered physically and emotionally through hunger and temptation. *Jesus doesn't condemn us when we're tempted to overeat or drink to fill the ache. Instead, He provides a better way. He says, "Come to me when you're burdened and weighed down with grief. I'll carry the load. You just rest."*

- Jesus experienced times of intense discouragement, sadness and grief. *He mourns with my husband and me over our son's mental illness and with you over your child's struggles. He understands how this discourages us and makes us sad.*

- Jesus loved the whole world and even died for everyone[8], but so many reject His love and do not love Him in return. Even His children too often take His love for granted and forget what it cost Him. *Jesus knows exactly how it feels when our kids don't reciprocate our love or say they hate us.*

The apostle Peter wrote, *"Dear friends, don't be surprised at the fiery trials you are going through, as if something strange were happening to you. Instead, be very glad—for these trials make you partners with Christ in his suffering, so that you will have the wonderful joy of seeing his glory when it is revealed to all the world"* (1 Peter 4:13, NLT).

An especially meaningful lesson Scripture teaches about suffering is that as God reaches out to comfort us, we in turn can then reach out and comfort others. *"God is our merciful Father and the source of all comfort. He comforts us in all our troubles so that we can comfort others. When they are troubled, we will be able to give them the same comfort God has given us. We are confident that the more you share in our sufferings, you will also share in the comfort God gives"* (2 Cor. 1:3b-5, 7, NLT).

Many parents interviewed conveyed beautiful stories of how God has enlarged their hearts to reach out and encourage other struggling parents. They realize that, because of their suffering and heartaches, they are uniquely able to minister to those in similar situations. In her timeless devotional *Streams in the Desert*, L.B. Cowman wisely discerned, "The ministry of *thorns* has often been a greater ministry to humankind than the ministry of *thrones*."[9] We will explore this ingenious truth in greater detail in Chapter 10.

Finally, it's vital to understand that when we relinquish our suffering to God, He is able to *redeem it* and *transform it* into good. A very familiar passage of Scripture is Romans 8:28-29: *"And we know that in all things God works for the good of those who love him, who have been called according to his purpose. For those God foreknew he also predestined to be conformed to the image of his Son"* (NIV). Another translation reads like this: *"We are confident that God is able to orchestrate everything to work toward something good and beautiful when we love Him and accept His invitation to live according to His plan. From the distant past, His eternal love reached into the future. You see, He knew those who would be His one day, and He chose them beforehand to be conformed to the image of His Son"* (VOICE).

God's ultimate end goal is for us to increasingly become more like Jesus in nature and character. Any time Satan brings suffering into our lives, God is able to redeem it and transform it into something of value in unique and creative ways. In essence, He "buys it back and exchanges it"[10] for something *good and beautiful,* as He works deep within us. And because of God's tender love for us, we can be assured that nothing of eternal value will be lost in the process of our transformation.

Satan has one purpose—death, by any means. He comes to steal, kill and destroy. With Jesus' help, however, we and our families will not be destroyed. You see, Jesus, too, has one purpose. He comes to bring life, abundant and full. And nothing in all creation—no suffering, no trials, not even mental illness—can separate us from the love of God we experience in Christ Jesus.

"If you have surrendered yourself to Christ, your present circumstances that seem to be pressing so hard against you are the perfect tool in the Father's hand to chisel you into shape for eternity. So trust Him and never push away the instrument He is using, or you will miss the result of His work in your life. The school of suffering graduates exceptional scholars."[11]

Additional Scripture to meditate on

*For the eyes of the Lord range throughout the earth to
strengthen those whose hearts are fully committed to him.
(2 Chronicles 16:9a, NIV)*

*In all their suffering, he also suffered,
and he personally rescued them,
In his love and mercy he redeemed them.
He lifted them up and carried them
through all the years. (Isaiah 63:9, NLT)*

*The thief approaches with malicious intent, looking to steal,
slaughter, and destroy; I came to give life with joy and abundance.
(John 10:10, VOICE)*

*This is the message we heard from Jesus and now declare to you:
God is light, and there is no darkness in him at all. (1 John 1:5, NLT)*

Prayer for God's transforming love

Loving Father, sometimes we're surprised by the level of suffering we and our children endure. Instead of blaming You, may we use these times to reach out to You and open our hearts to Your transforming love. We're so thankful for Your redeeming work on the cross. We praise You for Your ability to turn our suffering upside down and for Your promise to reconstruct every detail of our lives into something good. Give us the grace to live each day in the light of Your love. In the name of Jesus we pray. Amen.

GOING DEEPER—GETTING PERSONAL ————

1. Have you ever found yourself questioning or doubting the goodness of God during a time of suffering? What, if anything, helped you regain a perspective of God's innate goodness?

2. What key point on suffering resonated most deeply for you? Why?

3. Do you have a favorite go-to verse or passage you find yourself clinging to when you're in a place of suffering? If so, what is it? If not, which of the passages listed above (or in the previous chapter) do you find especially meaningful?

CHAPTER NINE

Church: Dealing With Our "No-Casserole Illnesses"

A GLIMPSE INSIDE

Church is hard. I feel like a fake at church and find myself hiding behind a façade. I can't say anything to anyone about Stacia's mental illness because she doesn't want me to. So no one knows. As I sit in the service, I often fight tears, especially during the songs. I so often want to just sit and cry, but others would be curious about what's wrong and I can't tell them. I wonder, though, if we could tell people, what would they think? How would they treat Stacia? How would they treat us? Would they think Stacia has this brain disorder because she (or we) did something wrong?

To be honest, this was by far the most difficult chapter to write. I love and respect the church and hold it in high esteem. The church is the body of Christ here on earth, and my intention is not to stand on a bully pulpit, pointing a critical finger. I'm painfully aware that I am guilty of committing many of the same offenses spelled out in this chapter. I've often been too wrapped up in the struggles of our own family to be sensitive to the challenges others in our church might be experiencing. Our own pain can make us intensely self-focused and cloud our vision to the pain of others.

But this is a discussion we need to have. No matter what denomination or flavor of church you identify with, you've likely been on both sides of the hurt. As a parent of a child with a mental or emotional disorder, chances are high you've been wounded by the treatment of others. As a member or regular attendee of a local church, chances are just as high you've done some wounding (no matter how unintentional) yourself.

For many of us, our church* is an integral part of our lives. Perhaps we even identify the place we worship each Sunday as our "church home" and the members with whom we worship as our "church family." But no family is perfect. Every home has issues within its walls, and there are times we offend and hurt one another. Unfortunately, many of our church families are no different. Terri, who is quoted in the first paragraph, has not shared their story with others in their church out of respect to her daughter's wishes. But she also hesitates to share because she fears the stigma surrounding mental illness. She is very aware that mental illness is not acceptable—not in the community and not in our churches. Terri is not alone in her fears. Many of the parents interviewed said they have

---

* *For this discussion, the word "church" is used to indicate a "body of Christians worshipping in a particular building or constituting one congregation" (definition from www.dictionary.com).*

not openly shared their struggles within the church because they fear a negative response.

When asked about their church experiences, the majority of the parents interviewed were, at best, ambivalent about their church family and, at worst, completely frustrated, disillusioned and even hurt by their churches. Terri is not far off in her fears of being misunderstood and judged if others found out about her daughter. It is heartbreaking that many parents do indeed experience this very thing as they struggle with their child's mental illness.

We want our churches to be places of refuge, comfort, hope and healing. We have an intense desire to know we matter to the members of our church fellowship. Yet for many of us who have a child living with mental and emotional health issues, our experiences within the local church have been very difficult—even painful. Amy Simpson, in her excellent book *Troubled Minds*, writes, "People with mental illness and their families—especially parents of children with mental illness—often feel condemned for their suffering. Instead of walking through the doors of the church to find the no-condemnation grace of Jesus, they find an assumption that they must have done something to deserve their suffering. They find a subtle expectation that they'd better fix themselves if they want to be part of a fellowship."[1]

And so we remain silent. We hesitate to share our deepest pain with those we should be able to trust the most. We long to be drawn in by love, but we fear we will be shunned and shamed.

Parent after parent had stories to tell about their experiences with their local churches. Some experiences were uplifting and encouraging, while others were disheartening. Many parents, on some level, understand why their church family reacts the way it does to them and their children, yet they wish the church was more helpful and empathetic to their needs. Many feel overlooked by their church family. They rightly acknowledge that if their child had cancer or some other serious physical illness or injury, the church members would do everything possible to offer help. Simpson puts it this way, "As we're busy enthusiastically delivering meals to suffering people, we are largely ignoring the afflictions of 25 percent of our population. That's about equal to the total percentage of people diagnosed with cancer each year, those living with heart disease, those infected with HIV and AIDS and those afflicted with diabetes—combined. No wonder people...call mental illness the 'no-casserole illness.' In contrast to the care we provide for others, we have very little patience with those whose diseases happen to attack their minds. And many people suffer in silence."[2]

Perhaps we need to take it even one step further and ask this probing question: Why is it that, in this age of mission trips and serve projects, we can reach out so lovingly and generously to strangers and completely miss the needs of many we rub shoulders with each Sunday?

Mother Teresa addressed that very thing when she said, "It is easier to love people far away. It is not always so easy to love those close to us. It is easier to give a cup of rice to relieve hunger than to relieve the loneliness and pain of someone unloved in our own home. Bring love into your home for this is where our love for each other must start."[3]

We need to tweak this quote just a bit and speak to our church families in this paraphrase:

> It is easier to love people far away. It is not always so easy to love those close to us. It is easier to go to a foreign, faraway country to give a cup of rice to relieve hunger, than to relieve the loneliness and pain of someone unloved in our own church. Bring love into your church home for this is where our love for each other must start.

Walt and Margaret have several children with a variety of special needs. Their church is well aware of their struggles, as Walt and Margaret have worked hard to educate their church family. They've tried to make their church aware of and more welcoming to those who struggle with mental illness, but Walt said, "No one seems to care. It feels at times as if we're beating our heads against a wall." Part of their frustration lies with seeing how their church has (rightly) made things easier and more accessible for those who have physical disabilities, such as installing elevators, wheelchair ramps, better sound systems, etc. Unfortunately, though, adaptations for mental health issues have been pushed aside. Margaret mentioned another factor. "All of our children look normal. They have invisible disabilities. This makes it more difficult for people to understand the issues we deal with every day. The tendency is for others to make comments such as, 'Why can't you control your children?' or 'Why can't those kids conduct themselves more properly?' Those comments hurt us. On the outside it might look like we're bad parents, and you may think our children's issues are a result of poor parenting. If you've not walked in our shoes, however, please offer us grace. Get to know us without making an instant judgment."

Gloria, a single mom, had hoped to find supportive friends at the new church she and her daughter began attending after a recent move. Her daughter, Cadence, has a variety of severe emotional health challenges due to early childhood abuse and trauma. Gloria stated that while a couple of her non-church friends have been fairly supportive, church members have been the least supportive. She said many in her church were extremely judgmental, which was very disappointing to her. In Gloria's words, "Even our pastor made it clear he didn't want his kids around Cadence. That was very hurtful for both of us."

Sophie's son, Alexander, needed to drop out of college after becoming very ill with schizophrenia. Sophie found it frustrating that initially so many blamed his illness on either the transition to college life or flat-out rebellion. "Early in Alexander's illness two church elders came to visit with him, as they felt he was simply being rebellious. People just didn't understand; they didn't view him as ill. It was disappointing to me and disheartening for Alexander. He felt like he couldn't live up to the expectations of others."

Stories like these are heartbreaking, and the families I spoke with have responded in a variety of ways. Many simply continue limping along in their churches, accepting that this is just how it is. Some families have switched churches and joined a church where they feel welcomed, accepted and understood. Others have been so disillusioned and hurt by their church experience they've dropped out of church altogether.

Other parents, however, have dared to share their struggles with their church families and have found safe havens of love and support within their churches. Rebecca is thankful for the prayer support she and her husband receive at their church. She is part of a prayer group made up of women who have adult children with similar challenges, and her husband is in a comparable prayer group for men. The groups meet once a month to share their burdens and encourage each other in prayer.

Vanessa said her daughter, Sierra, age seven, loves to go to church. Sierra has a diagnosis of early-onset bipolar disorder, anxiety disorder and sensory processing disorder. The children's pastor at their church is aware of Sierra's struggles and she is, according to Vanessa, "just wonderful!" Vanessa and her husband, Rory, have been open about their challenges with Sierra with their small group and have found the members to be compassionate and helpful.

Several parents said they felt free to call their pastors or church leaders when they needed specific prayers for their child or themselves. One mom mentioned that her church offers Christian formation classes for children with special needs, and another said their church helps those with special needs understand and participate in communion. A few parents expressed their appreciation that their churches offer Bible studies or support groups specifically for parents who have children with special needs. Many others said they had friends within their church who, even if they didn't completely understand their struggles, were empathetic, encouraging and supportive.

Regardless of the challenges we face with our children, we all long to be treated with love and respect by others in the church. We want to know we matter to those with whom we sit in the church pews each week. We have a heartfelt need to know we and our children are accepted as valued members by this body of believers.

GAZING UP

"The way God designed our bodies is a model for understanding our lives together as a church: every part dependent on every other part, the parts we mention and the parts we don't, the parts we see and the parts we don't. If one part hurts, every other part is involved in the hurt, and in the healing. If one part flourishes, every other part enters into the exuberance. You are Christ's body—that's who you are! You must never forget this" (1 Cor. 12:25-27, MSG).

Deanna defines herself as "one tired mom." Her young son, Evan, was recently diagnosed with autism spectrum disorder. She chose to homeschool Evan for his kindergarten year, and she readily admits there are days she's simply exhausted by Evan's meltdowns, his fixations and his obsessions. "Evan's personality," states Deanna, "is a double-edged sword. Things can go from calm to tears in a heartbeat."

When asked about her experience within their local church fellowship, Deanna said their church family was, for the most part, helpful and not too judgmental. Their church is well-aware of Evan's autism, and his Sunday school teachers have been very helpful, even providing a one-on-one aide for Evan. She said some members of the church, hoping to be encouraging and helpful, have given them articles about autism. But what touched her heart most deeply was receiving a note from an older woman in their church who shared some very difficult issues they had with their own child in his growing-up years. This kind woman shared her *heart*, offering Deanna and her husband some much-appreciated encouragement and understanding.

Dawn and Tony are thrilled that their church has assigned a one-on-one associate for their young son during the morning worship service. "What I love most about this arrangement," Dawn shared, "is that it enables us to peacefully enjoy the worship service together with our other children. We no longer have to tag team going to church. This works well in our church because there are multiple services, so no one is missing worship. Our associate attends one service and then is free to watch our son while we attend a later service. Another thing we appreciate is that, from a safety perspective, we are all in the same building. If there was a medical or behavioral emergency, we'd be right there."

Regardless of what we have or have not experienced in our churches, the reality is that most of our churches are neither all good nor all bad. In all likelihood our experiences will fall into the both/

and category. It is probable that we will be blessed with empathy and understanding from some in our churches and receive judgement and criticism from others.

How can churches be a blessing to families like ours? What are families longing for? Here are four suggestions that rose to the surface when this question was posed to the parents interviewed:

1. **A listening ear:** *"To respond to a matter before you hear about it shows foolishness and brings shame"* (Prov. 18:13, VOICE).

When parents whose children are struggling with emotional health issues dare step out of the shadows to share what they're dealing with in their homes, it's crucial they know they are being *listened to and believed.* Parents yearn to be taken seriously. They long for their church families—beginning with the leadership—to offer hope and encouragement; to respond with grace, not judgment. It hurts when others deny their experiences or minimize their distress. It's demeaning when others issue glib advice or offer a "magic bullet" that promises an instant cure. Robert Albers and William Meller, in their book *Ministry With Persons With Mental Illness and Their Families,* write, "It is (our) conviction that people are not so much looking for answers as they are looking for understanding."[4]

Margot honestly states, "I appreciate it when people ask how I'm doing and then really listen to what I say—simply listen and empathize with me. I'm not looking for advice or asking them to fix it! In fact, I find myself getting defensive when others offer pat advice or tired clichés or make suggestions about what our child *really* needs. I have a hard time knowing how to respond when I'm told we should try this vitamin or that oil or go to their chiropractor, etc. Unless they are a mental health professional working with our family, I wish they wouldn't offer advice. It just adds another level of confusion and disquietude to an already emotional situation."

One of the things Kris appreciated most about her church during their son's difficult growing-up years was that their pastor's wife was such a good listener and was willing to spend time with her. "All of the sermons in the world didn't touch me as much as having this dear friend simply come alongside me, listening and caring. She didn't try to offer advice or give me books to read or tell me what I should do. She just listened and cared and prayed. She was simply there."

Having a child diagnosed with a mental or emotional health disorder ushers parents into a season of grief. As we discussed in Chapter 4, our seasons of grief are not once and done. It's not unusual for parents to cycle in and out of periods of sadness and grief, even if it has been many years since their child's first episode. As parents, our desire is for others to listen to our pain and simply allow us to grieve—no matter how old our child is. The reality is that most parents who have a child with a brain disorder will continue to experience episodes of grief long into their child's adulthood.

2. **Listen—and follow through:** *"Dear children, let's not merely say that we love each other; let us show the truth by our actions" (1 John 3:18, NLT).*

When families approach the leadership in their church to ask for specific help, the church should do all it can to provide the requested support (within reason). Families are disheartened and hurt when their needs and requests are largely ignored. They receive the message that their children are not worth the extra effort—they are too much trouble, too difficult, too needy. This was precisely the message Bruce and Rhonda received after asking for help with their teenage daughter.

Bruce and Rhonda's daughter, Brianna, was deeply hurt by her youth group experience. Brianna struggles with a mood disorder that leads to poor impulse control, poor judgment, social anxiety and defiance. Bruce and Rhonda tried to explain their daughter's issues to their church's youth pastor and gave him some specific ideas of how he could be helpful, but it was obvious he didn't quite know what to do with Brianna. Bruce and Rhonda felt the youth pastor and other youth group leaders did not treat Brianna well, nor did they try to make her feel included or valued. Brianna dropped out of her youth group soon after the year began. Rhonda painfully shared, "The whole youth group episode added to our sense of isolation and aloneness. If only one of the leaders had tried to connect with Brianna—tried to get an understanding of how she viewed life, listened to her struggles, learned what she enjoys—it could have made a huge difference."

3. **Practical support:** *"Carry each other's burdens, and in this way you will fulfill the law of Christ"* *(Gal. 6:2, NIV).*

Oftentimes, it's the little things that count. As parents of children with some pretty difficult challenges and needs, we long for our church family to understand and care enough to reach out and offer help. Mother Teresa succinctly stated, "Not all of us can do great things. But we can do small things with great love."[5] There are so many practical "small things of great love" our churches can do that would help bear our burdens.

Lora is deeply appreciative about the support they've received from their church family. They have an adult son in his forties who lives with them. Marc has a variety of mental and emotional health issues, along with some significant physical challenges. A few men in their church are very helpful with Marc. They drive him to appointments, take him out for rides, help him with computer issues, come visit him, etc. The pastors in their church have also been supportive, and they, too, visit Marc on a regular basis. Each act of kindness helps lighten the load for Lora and her husband.

Vicky enthusiastically said, "My church offers a night out for parents who have children with special needs. Child care is included! This gives us a rare evening away, with the added benefit of not having to ask my parents to watch Grayson. This is huge for us! Since Grayson, who has autism spectrum disorder, is such a handful, we've lost most of our other babysitters."

Pamela and Stan long for their church to help out in practical ways with their adult daughter, Melanie, who struggles with autism, a variety of learning disabilities and sensory issues. Melanie enjoys going to church and has even gone on a few short-term mission trips with church members. Pamela said that even though their church is accepting of Melanie, they only connect with her on Sundays. "What about Monday through Saturday? Melanie is lonely and would love someone to spend time with her. She could use help organizing and cleaning her apartment, help with her finances, etc. Stan and I help her in these areas, but it would be such a Godsend if a few others would reach out to Melanie in her day-to-day living. This would not only lift some of the burden from us, it would be such a boost to Melanie. She desperately needs a friend or two."

Several parents mentioned they wish someone would offer to spend time with their son or daughter one on one—to make some sort of connection to help break their isolation. They would especially appreciate others taking the initiative. One single mom told me she always has to ask others for help. Even though most are willing, she wishes that occasionally someone would volunteer on their own.

4. **Spiritual help:** *"Encourage the disheartened, help the weak, be patient with everyone. Pray continually" (1 Thess. 5:14b, 17, NIV).*

Michelle appreciates the support her family receives from their church. "I've called the elders to come pray with and for our daughter who struggles with a severe mood disorder. They don't really know what else to do to help us, but they do care about us. This is abundantly evident in their heartfelt prayers for us."

Rebecca had an honest discussion with her pastor and asked him to remember to include those who struggle with mental or emotional challenges in his corporate prayers. "Our pastor always prayed for those who were hospitalized or homebound due to physical illnesses, but he never thought to pray for those whose illnesses were unseen. I simply asked him to pray (in general) for those struggling with mental illness or emotional disorders."

Parents who have children with severe emotional challenges walk a very lonely, isolated and often confusing road. They appreciate a pastor, a member of the prayer ministry, a church leader or simply a fellow member coming alongside them and praying with them regarding the struggles they're experiencing. Praying together—or having someone pray for us—reminds us that we are not alone in this battle. Perhaps there's not much else others can do for us, but prayers are always powerful! After all, "Prayer is not a substitute for action; it is an action for which there is no substitute."[6]

Yes, life is messy and often complicated—life in the church is no different. We would do well, however, to go back to Church 101 and follow the basic laws of love:

- Love God and love others.
- Act justly, love mercy and walk humbly with God.
- Treat others as you wish to be treated.

"So speak encouraging words to one another. Build up hope so you'll all be together in this, no one left out, no one left behind. I know you're already doing this; just keep on doing it" (1 Thess. 5:11, MSG).

Additional Scripture to meditate on

"The most important commandment," answered Jesus, "is this…'Love the Lord your God with all your heart and with all your soul and with all your mind and with all your strength.' The second is this: 'Love your neighbor as yourself.' There is no commandment greater than these." (Mark 12:29-31, NIV)

…What does the Lord require of you? To act justly and to love mercy and to walk humbly with your God. (Micah 6:8, NIV)

This is what our Scriptures come to teach: in everything, in every circumstance, do to others as you would have them do to you. (Matt. 7:12, VOICE)

My little children, don't just talk about love as an idea or theory. Make it your true way of life, and live in the pattern of gracious love. (1 John 3:18, VOICE)

A prayer for healing and grace

Lord Jesus, this is a hard one. Many of us have been hurt by our church families. As parents, we've too often experienced judgment and criticism instead of love and understanding. Bring healing to our hearts and fill us with grace and forgiveness for those who simply don't understand our journey. We pray, Jesus, for our churches. Help us all to *live in the pattern of gracious love*. We ask that You move hearts to relieve the loneliness and pain of those within our church fellowship. Your desire, Jesus, is for us to *do what is right and to love mercy*. May we build each other up, love without condition and leave no one wandering alone in the dark shadows of our churches. May we not merely say that we love each other, but may we show this truth by our actions. As You have loved us, Jesus, help us love one another. In Your name we pray. Amen.

GOING DEEPER—GETTING PERSONAL ──────────

1. Have you ever talked to your pastor, a church leader, or any others in your church about your challenges with your child? If so, what has been their response? If not, what has kept you from sharing?

2. What are some "small things of great love" your church has done for your family? Can you share some ways they have helped you bear your burdens, either practically or spiritually?

3. Do you have any specific suggestions—a wish list—you would like to share with your church leadership?

CHAPTER TEN

When Satan Intends Evil: Treasures Unearthed from Darkness

A GLIMPSE INSIDE

"I will give you treasures hidden in the darkness—secret riches. I will do this so you may know that I am the Lord, the God of Israel, the one who calls you by name" (Isaiah 45:3, NLT).

Treasures hidden in the darkness—secret riches. We've touched on this concept frequently throughout this book. Yet it bears looking at more closely. So often, in the midst of our difficult day-to-day challenges, we just can't see it. What treasures could possibly be hidden in the chaos of chronic mental illness and the darkness that so often surrounds it?

We were thrust into one of the darkest seasons of our lives when Kyle, as a young adult, decided he no longer needed his medication. We felt helpless and powerless as we watched our son plunge deep into psychosis. We suspected he was making some very poor choices, but because he was an adult—and because of how the laws were written—we were limited in what we could do for him. We knew he desperately needed help, but his illness prevented him from recognizing the need. We also knew he would eventually hit bottom and feared what that would look like.

The night our son was arrested we discovered just how dark and frightening it is at the bottom.

The morning after our son's arrest, I remember sitting on our deck and crying out to God. Steve had gone to get Kyle and arrange bail. I had spent most of the morning calling family and friends, letting them know what happened—and most importantly, asking for their prayers. When I had a few moments, I grabbed a glass of iced tea and went out to my deck. *What good could ever come out of this?* I cried in anguish to God. *None of this makes any sense—especially not for Kyle. I know You can use anything to better strengthen my faith—even this, but please don't throw Kyle under the bus to do so! Don't sacrifice him to grow me.*

As I wept to the Lord, I felt His peace surround me. He reminded me of His self-description—who He is and how He acts toward His children. *"The LORD, the LORD, the compassionate and gracious God, slow to anger, abounding in love and faithfulness"* (Ex. 34:6-7a). Compassionate, gracious, not easily angered, overflowing with love, faithful. *This* is who our Lord is. God does not throw one person under the bus to grow another. God generously lavishes love—not harm—on His children.

When God extends Satan's leash—allowing pain and suffering to invade our lives—it's important to keep our eyes on Jesus. Satan relishes chaos, diabolically hoping to sow evil and destruction. But God has an amazing way of turning things right-side up. If we could pull back the veil that separates the physical world from the spiritual world, we would have a much clearer understanding of things. In our limited, linear perspective, we always expect that A plus B will equal C. God, however, doesn't limit Himself to working as we expect. In our human reasoning, we can't possibly fathom why

God would allow our children to suffer from mental illness and all its ramifications—and allow us to suffer right along with them. Yet, as we discussed in the previous chapters on suffering, God sees and knows things we can't begin to comprehend.

In the midst of the murkiness, it's important to keep one thing clear: God always has a plan. A plan to bring good, even from Satan's intent to bring evil.

Fast-forward eight difficult months after Kyle's arrest. Though things were falling into place for Kyle, I still struggled with wondering why God had allowed this to happen and what good could possibly come out of it. Because of our son's poor choices—which we firmly believe stemmed from his underlying mental illness—his life was forever changed in some very significant ways. And that broke my heart. One morning, however, after listening to a video blog about "flipping the switch" to see things from God's perspective, I asked God how *He* saw this situation with Kyle. As I prayed about it, God seemed to clarify some things. He reminded me of the good that had already come about. Kyle was once again under the care of a psychiatrist and back on medication. He had recently moved out of our home into to a highly supervised group home and was setting some positives goals for his future. God specifically impressed on my heart how beneficial and necessary the boundaries were that had been placed firmly around my son. He reminded me that Kyle will have the opportunity to thrive and flourish as he lives a more disciplined, scheduled life, even if he chafes under the structure for a while. God graciously gave me a small glimpse into how He is able to take something Satan intended for evil and destruction and mold it into something good and beneficial—not only for Kyle, but for us as well.

The thing about "molding," though, is that it's usually quite painful. It hurts to be pulled and pounded and stretched. Oswald Chambers likens it to being a bow and arrow in the hands of God: "A saint's life is in the hands of God like a bow and arrow in the hands of the archer. God is aiming at something the saint cannot see, but our Lord continues to stretch and strain, and every once in a while the saint says, 'I cannot take any more.' Yet God pays no attention; He goes on stretching until His purpose is in sight, then He lets the arrow fly."[1]

As God shapes us, He focuses His mind's eye on something we can't yet discern. While we see only what's in front of us—the pain of our present circumstances—God sees so much more. As God molds, stretches and pulls us, we really have no idea what the finished product will look like—and we definitely can't imagine anything beautiful being formed from our present reality. In fact, as we wrestle with our child's mental illness diagnosis—and all the pain, anguish and chaos that accompanies it—there may be times we wonder if we'll actually be destroyed in the process.

Yet we need never wrestle without hope! The enduring hope we have is that God is love and His plans for His children are always good. He has the amazing ability to redeem anything—even the pain and suffering we and our children experience—and use it to create something of immense value. Even though we may never get to the point of being thankful for our child's mental health disorder and challenges, we may reach the point of seeing some of the good God intended when He allowed our child to be inflicted with such difficulties.

Perhaps we need to look for the treasures that are hidden.

As a little girl, I loved *Highlights* magazine. Each month I eagerly looked forward to the hidden pictures feature! I intently examined the pages and loved the satisfaction of finding a previously unseen picture hidden in the most unlikely of places. And once spotted, it became so obvious. The true image was there all along!

Sometimes, the truest image is hidden in the clutter of the surrounding chaos.

In Genesis 50:20, Joseph told his brothers who, years before, had callously sold him into slavery, *"You intended to harm me, but God intended it for good to accomplish what is now being done"* (NIV). Satan always intends death; in fact, his sole purpose is to steal, kill and destroy, and he will use whatever means he can to accomplish this. Jesus, however, came to bring LIFE—beautiful, abundant and full. So, when Satan smears the dark paint of chaos and gloom over the picture of our life, God wants us to search for and reclaim the beauty of our identity and purpose. He promises that, even in the dark, there are secret riches and hidden treasures to be found.

Many courageous parents who have children with severe mental health challenges can attest to the abundance of beautiful ways God has taken what Satan intended for evil and turned it—or is turning it—into valuable treasure.

GAZING UP

"You intended to harm me, but God intended it for good to accomplish what is now being done." After referencing these words from Genesis 50:20, parents were asked the question, "Can you identify any positives that have come out of this journey you're on?" As parents shared the ways they've seen God bring good from their pain, five key points came to light.

The number-one answer parents gave was that in the midst of such challenging hardships, they were blessed with a much closer, much stronger relationship with God.

"I would have to say," Carol shared, "that all the adversity and all the pain we've experienced on our journey with Max has definitely drawn me closer to God. My relationship with God is much deeper and richer than it's ever been. I depend on Him more than ever."

Carol's sentiment was echoed by most of the parents I interviewed.

Rita said, "To be honest, it's sort of hard to think of positives that have come out of Barry's severe, chronic depression, at least not for him…not yet, anyway. But as for me, my relationship with God has grown so much. God has greatly increased my trust. Without this experience I wouldn't understand how big God is. I *know* God is always there for us—no matter what."

Kent and Steph, whose daughter, Lainie, has fetal alcohol syndrome, as well as Asperger's, agreed. "We have definitely grown closer to the Lord and to each other. We've learned new and deeper ways of relying more fully on God. Only God could take something so awful and turn it into something good. We've seen miracles in Lainie's life that have greatly increased our faith."

A second positive many parents testified to was how God was using their adversity to *change them*. These parents shared a variety of ways they feel they've been reshaped because of their child's emotional disorder or mental illness.

"As we've walked with Haley through the extreme highs and lows of her life," Brad recounted, "we've learned some very hard lessons in TRUST. God has been faithfully teaching us to trust Him; to relinquish and release those things to Him over which we have no control. As a business executive, I'm used to leading and taking charge. However, I now see there are things that are completely beyond my control. As Scripture points out, some things are beyond human reasoning. I'm slowly learning to let go."

"Our family does not look anything like we thought it would," admitted Rebecca. "But in a very real sense, it's much better this way. I believe both Dan and I are more Christ-like because of the journey we've been on with Tyler. We're more empathetic and less judgmental, more patient and less intolerant. We've seen tangible ways God has used our difficult journey with Tyler to change us and our family for the better. Satan wanted to destroy our family with mental illness, despair, discouragement and hopelessness, but God is using that very thing to redeem, transform and change us!"

Liz feels like her personality has changed due to her daughter, Beth's, schizophrenia. "I was always kind of serious, but I've learned to lighten up a little! Beth makes me look at life from a completely different perspective, since she interprets the world so uniquely. I'm learning to see life through different eyes."

Many parents mentioned that the pain and the struggles they've experienced along the way have given them a heart for those who deal with similar issues. Other parents realized they were learning to prioritize their time better. Still others acknowledged they were allowing God to make them "better, not bitter" and were more understanding of those who have similar mental health struggles. One mom expressed that, by nature, she's more of an intellectual and wasn't always so comfortable dealing in the emotional realm. "Now I've become more aware and observant of emotional issues and how to best deal with them. I'm more in-tune with others who are suffering." Several parents recognize that their child's issues have forced them to become much more assertive; they are now strong advocates for their children and for others who struggle with mental illness. A few parents admitted that their child's diagnosis gave them the motivation to deal with *their own* mental health issues. And one honest mom said, "In my younger years, I enjoyed being around and working with people who have disabilities, but I never wanted to be the mom of one. Thankfully, God has turned this around! He has definitely worked in my heart and changed my thinking."

A third positive many parents acknowledged was the realization that God has taken the difficult journey they are on and has transformed it into a *ministry* of some sort. They're able to see that the very thing that has caused them so much pain and conflict has been used by God to intentionally help and bless others. The late Dr. Adrian Rogers[2] once stated, "Jesus had some scars, and if you follow him, so will you. Your scars may be your greatest ministry."

Marie's son, Carson, is in his late teens. Carson, who has a diagnosis of bipolar disorder and ADHD, is currently living in a long-term residential facility. Marie emphatically stated, "I spent ten difficult, painful years fighting to get the necessary care and intervention for my son. When we were told we may need to abandon our rights as parents to get help for Carson, I was astounded. This should NEVER be the only card left for parents. That is NOT acceptable! That mindset spurred me to go to the top of the mental health bureaucracies to advocate for our son." Eventually, Marie helped start a foundation for parents who find themselves in similar situations. Marie said, "Our foundation serves as a strong advocate for families in mental health crises. We do things like go to school meetings with the parents, raise funds, provide meals and offer other practical help for families in crisis. We also speak at churches and community events about mental health initiatives."

Kimberly, a family-law attorney who has a daughter with anti-social personality disorder, often finds herself offering support and encouragement to parents in similar circumstances. She actively seeks ways to help and serve others in her role as an attorney.

Parents shared about support groups formed; careers chosen; care ministries implemented; books, blogs and articles written; prayer groups organized; and deep friendships formed as a direct result of having a child with severe, chronic mental health challenges. Indeed, much life-giving fruit has grown out of what many parents would define as their greatest sorrow.

A fourth positive several parents mentioned is being played out in the lives of their *other children*. Like ripples on a pond, the effects of having a child in the family who struggles with a severe emotional disorder reaches further than the parents. Each member of the family is impacted in a profound way. While it's common to look at the negative impact mental illness has on our families, many parents shared some *positive* ways their other children were being shaped. Parents have seen how, even in the midst of the turmoil, angst and embarrassment their troubled child often brings to the home, God has used this very adversity to help shape their other children in some wonderful ways.

Luke and Patti adopted a group of four siblings after being their foster parents for several months. Each child has some significant challenges and delays, but Henry, in particular, struggles the most profoundly. His predominate mood is anger—he lies without flinching, he's manipulative and defiant, he's volatile and brings much chaos to the home. The tumult he brings has destroyed any semblance of peace and order their family once enjoyed. This has been very difficult—not just for Luke and Patti, but for their three biological children as well. The three older children remember how things used to be...*before*. Yet, even in the midst of the discord, Luke and Patti have seen how their biological children are changing—in many ways for the better. Patti noted, "Our older bio kids have had to mature and grow up. I now see them mentoring other kids. Our kids are protective and caring, even in the midst of the embarrassment and frustration."

Colleen and Jeff intuitively know their grown sons are watching them parent their youngest child. "It's been a blessing to see how our sons and daughters-in-law are parenting their children with love and grace. They've had a front-row seat as they've watched us struggle through the challenges with their younger sister. They see we haven't given up on her. They see our deep and committed love. And now WE see how they've been shaped and molded in part by watching us."

Vicki said her children are learning how to have compassionate hearts because of their brother's challenges. She stated, "I still often ask God to heal Grayson. However, I do think that whatever He does—whether He chooses to heal Grayson or not—will benefit all my kids in the long term. I'm already seeing this being played out in their lives. They are much more understanding and empathetic due to life with Grayson!"

We will look more closely at the effect of mental health disorders on sibling relationships in Chapter 14.

And finally, a fifth beautiful positive some parents recounted was how they've seen their struggling child grow and develop in unique ways—ways directly tied to their emotional challenges. Parents shared the humble gratification of seeing their child embrace their identity as they become the person God created them to be. Their victories and accomplishments may look very different from what the world considers success, but as parents we have firsthand knowledge of the difficulties they've encountered along the way. We've intimately seen the challenges that have plagued and assailed our children, not only from within their own minds but also from a multitude of outside sources. And precisely *because* of their mental and emotional challenges, many of our children exhibit beautiful understanding and compassion for others who face similar struggles.

Lisa said, "I believe God will use Ashley somehow, in some profound way, due to her autism. She is a beautiful young lady—already so compassionate. I know God will continue to develop her strengths."

Anna is often impressed with the incredible giftedness of her son, Lucas, who struggles with ADHD. "I have heard and seen much of his creativity, his heart, all he has to offer, and it blesses me."

Patti, for all of their struggles with Henry, was deeply touched when he wrote a letter to his birthmother. He told her he forgave her and that he wants her to know God. She could see how God was already working in Henry's young heart, showing him the way of forgiveness and grace.

Yes, we live in a fallen world in which mental illness frequently delivers pain and chaos to our front door. And while it's true that pain *hurts* and chaos brings *confusion*, we need not allow Satan to have the last word. For every evil plan of Satan, God has a stunning plan of redemption. As we have discussed and discovered time and again, God has a fascinating way of creating beautiful treasures in the darkness of unfathomable challenges. And arching like a rainbow of promise over all our difficulties is God's ultimate end goal: to make us more and more like His Son, Jesus Christ. So God invites us to look for the hidden treasure being formed in our lives. As we look beneath the surface of our adversity, we are given the pleasure of unearthing treasure that was created uniquely for us—treasures mined from the darkest recesses of our pain, treasures that help us step more fully into the man or woman God sees us to be.

As believers, our greatest hope is found in the promise of our ultimate redemption. One day, every wrong will be made right, every pain replaced with joy and every last vestige of chaos restored to shalom. But even here—even on this side of heaven—God is able to take *anything* Satan intends for evil and create a masterpiece of beauty.

"We are confident that God is able to orchestrate everything to work toward something good and beautiful when we love Him and accept His

invitation to live according to His plan. From the distant past, His eternal love reached into the future. You see, He knew those who would be His one day, and He chose them beforehand to be conformed to the image of His Son...As for those He chose beforehand, He called them to a different destiny so that they would experience what it means to be made right with God and share in His glory" (Romans 8:28-30, VOICE).

Additional Scripture to meditate on

Let me hear of your unfailing love each morning,
    for I am trusting you.
Show me where to walk,
    for I give myself to you. (Psalm 143:8, NLT)

This happened so the powers of God could be seen...We must carry out the task assigned us by the One who sent us. (John 9:3-4, NLT)

For you are a chosen people...God's very own possession. As a result, you can show others the goodness of God, for he called you out of the darkness into his wonderful light. (1 Peter 2:9, NLT)

I am confident of this, that he who began a good work in you will carry it on to completion until the day of Christ Jesus. (Phil. 1:6, NIV)

God can do anything, you know—far more than you could ever imagine or guess or request in your wildest dreams! He does it not by pushing us around but by working within us, his Spirit deeply and gently within us. Glory to God...! (Eph. 3:20, MSG)

Prayer of praise for God's creative plan

Lord Jesus, thank You for Your holy reminder that there is beauty and treasure and abundance being formed even now in the darkness of our situations. Give us eyes to see in the dark. Show us the ways You are shaping and changing us. Reveal how You've equipped us and highlight the unique gifts You've given us. Open our eyes to see the surprising ways You're taking those very things Satan hoped would destroy us, and from them creating masterpieces of beauty. We love You, Jesus, and we know You can do immeasurably more than we could ask or imagine, according to Your power that is working deep within us. We humbly pray in Your name. Amen.

GOING DEEPER—GETTING PERSONAL ────────

1. Echoing Joseph's sentiment in Gen. 50:20—*"God intended for good to accomplish what is now being done"*—can you identify any good that has come out of the journey you're on with your child? If so, what is it?

2. How have you been changed or reshaped because of your child's mental health challenges?

3. What dreams do you have for your child? For yourself? How can you pray into those?

CHAPTER ELEVEN

Rising Above: Focusing on Jesus in the Midst of the Messiness

A GLIMPSE INSIDE

The story was once told of an elderly woman who had been widowed for several years. Miss Agnes met her husband when they were both quite young; they married when she was seventeen and he nineteen. Within a few years they had three precious sons, one of whom was born with cerebral palsy. Neither Agnes nor her husband were believers when they married. Miss Agnes was introduced to Jesus by a neighbor who invited her to church. Her husband was okay with that, as long as she didn't expect *him* to start attending church. Eventually though, the prayers of Agnes—and the pursuit of Jesus—won out and her husband, too, became a strong believer. When they were in their late twenties, her husband told Agnes he believed the Lord was calling them into full-time ministry. They planted a church in a downtown neighborhood of their city, and the next two decades were ones of unbelievable growth. The church grew and expanded beyond their wildest imaginations. They were sold out for Jesus!

When her husband was in his early forties, he was killed in a tragic accident. Not long after that, her son, who had cerebral palsy, also died. Miss Agnes was plunged into the deepest grief and darkest despair imaginable. For several months she was unable to rise above her loss and her faith was deeply shaken. Then one day Agnes clearly heard Jesus speak to her: "Your husband and your son are not the reason you live. I am the reason you live." He then encouraged her to climb out of the pit she was in and begin *living* again.

As Jesus healed her wounded soul, He began a new work in her heart. Miss Agnes realized she had made an idol of her husband—and even of his death—and had slowly allowed her grief to drive a wedge between herself and Jesus. She could see no future for herself since her husband and their ministry were gone. Jesus, however, saw a different picture.

Miss Agnes permitted Jesus to paint her life in a new way. She fell in love with Him all over again and truly allowed Jesus to be her reason for living. By the time she was in her mid-eighties, Miss Agnes had made well over fifty trips to faraway countries, sharing the Good News of Jesus. She said, "The second half of my life has been even sweeter than the first half."[1]

"The second half of my life has been even sweeter than the first half." When I first heard this, I wondered how that was possible. It seemed almost disloyal to her husband and son that Agnes would say life became "even sweeter" after they were gone.

However, by the time she reached her golden years, Miss Agnes was able to see a more complete picture. She had loved her husband and son with her whole heart. She and her husband had a rich, fulfilling life serving the Lord together, and she had enjoyed nurturing and caring for her son. Of course she grieved their deaths. But the time came for her to rise above the grief and pain—to thrive, not merely survive. She knew the question she ultimately had to answer was, "Is Jesus enough?" Could she look up from the emptiness of her life and focus on the fullness of Jesus and His love for her? Or would she only love Him when life was as she thought it should be? The point Miss Agnes was making was that Jesus was her reason for living. Because she had Jesus, she was satisfied and life was, indeed, sweet.

When life doesn't make sense and we find ourselves in a deep pit, can we say the same thing? Can we rise above our expectations and allow Jesus to be our reason for living?

How well I remember singing the praise song "You Are My All In All."[2]

You are my strength when I am weak
You are the treasure that I seek
You are my all in all.
Seeking You as a precious jewel
Lord, to give up I'd be a fool
You are my all in all.

Jesus, Lamb of God
Worthy is Your name.
Jesus, Lamb of God
Worthy is Your name.

This song is easy to sing and beautiful to harmonize, but in reality very difficult to live out. Yes, we want Jesus to be our all-in-all, but too often we want it on our terms. On Sunday, we joyfully declare that Jesus is the "treasure that we seek," but Monday comes and we find ourselves angry and frustrated by how our lives are playing out. Life stinks and we're unhappy.

It's hard dealing with the ugliness of mental illness. It saps our strength, shreds our emotions and threatens to destroy our families. We want our lives to be sweet and satisfying, but how can they be when it's just so painful? We have such expectations of what we want our families to look like, what we want our lives to look like. Then we get slammed with the reality that our child has autism or bipolar disorder or struggles with a personality disorder. We can barely breathe.

How can we possibly say, like Miss Agnes, that "life is sweet" after our world has been rocked with mental illness? What, really, does it look like to focus on Jesus and allow Him to be our satisfaction, our all-in-all, our very reason for living?

Rob and Susanna's son, Mac, was adopted at age seven from another country. Life in his biological home was very difficult and often filled with danger and upheaval. As an impressionable little boy, he witnessed and experienced untold horrors and was eventually placed in an orphanage. In time, Mac was adopted into a loving new home with parents and siblings who welcomed him with open arms and open hearts. Rob and Susanna felt incredibly blessed to receive this precious boy into their home. Mac's new home—clean, safe, warm and loving— was in complete contrast with the home of his birth. However, the trauma that marked his early life created much emotional damage, and Mac was eventually diagnosed with childhood PTSD.

From the start of their new life together, things were challenging. Mac found it difficult to assimilate into his strange new environment. Learning a new language, along with its idioms and colloquialisms, was especially problematic. In his frustration and confusion, Mac often acted out. He tested the boundaries and frequently clashed with his parents and others.

The summer before Mac's senior year in high school was especially tumultuous. Mac rebelled against any and all rules, ran away and eventually dropped out of school. He moved in with a drug dealer, and Mac's life was once again fraught with danger and upheaval—but this time by his own choice. Though Rob and Susanna were heartbroken by their son's destructive pursuits, their faith remained strong. "God gave me such peace throughout that whole awful summer," Susanna shared. "As He enveloped me in peace, He often reminded me to keep my focus on Him."

Mac is now in his mid-twenties and difficulties in his life persist. He struggles with relationships, often burning bridges between himself, his family and friends. He has trouble holding down a job and battles poor health. Though Mac would be welcomed to live in his parents' home, he prefers living in the midst of chaos, squalor and poverty.

Life with their son continues to be stormy and disruptive, but Rob and Susanna are choosing to keep their eyes on Jesus, looking to Him and living for Him. Susanna said she daily experiences the peace of God, knowing she and Rob are doing what they can for Mac. With the grace of Jesus nourishing them, they are able to love their son with a love that is generally not appreciated or reciprocated. And because they have learned to rise above their adversity, they are able to more clearly see the pain of others and respond to their needs. Susanna, with her huge heart and generous compassion, freely shares her time and love with many other hurting, wounded souls. She keeps her eyes on Jesus. He is her reason for living.

GAZING UP

I waited patiently for the LORD;
  he turned to me and heard my cry.
He lifted me out of the slimy pit,

out of the mud and mire;
he set my feet on a rock
  and gave me a firm place to stand.
He put a new song in my mouth,
  a hymn of praise to our God.
(Psalm 40:1-3a, NIV)

When we find ourselves in the messiness of life, deep in a pit of despair, we often discover Jesus pulls us out of that pit in surprising, unexpected ways. In our own reasoning, we have it all figured out. If only Jesus would heal my child, then I'll be happy again. Or, if only we could find the right psychiatric meds…or a successful residential program…or the perfect therapist, then everything would be okay. We'd get our joy back. If only…then. Too often we tend to focus exclusively on our circumstances, begging God to change them. God, though, would rather change us, and He often chooses to keep our circumstances unchanged.

Rebecca, the mom of a young man with schizophrenia, acknowledges that as her son got older, his mental illness went from bad to worse. Though she has deep faith and prays persistently for her son, Rebecca testifies, "God still has not healed our son's mental illness. In fact, things are worse today than they've ever been. But, God has changed me! I am much more dependent on Him, much more patient. I'm learning what it looks like to truly 'let go and let God.' Daily, I pray a prayer of relinquishment, releasing my son into God's loving hands. When I try to control things or allow my mind to stew and worry about our circumstances, I become anxious and fearful, full of doubt and despair. That's when God gently steps in and reminds me to keep my eyes on Him, not on our circumstances. God IS sovereign, even over our son's mental illness and all the junk that comes with it."

If we look at the short passage above from Psalm 40, we see that David, the Psalmist, cried out to the Lord. He didn't just complain to other people, he brought his complaints directly to God. David realized he was stuck in the mud and mire of his surroundings, and he knew the Lord was the only one who could pull him out of that pit. We also see that he was patient. David didn't demand God change his circumstances RIGHT NOW. Instead, he chose to wait patiently for God to answer—trusting in God's timing and praising Him in the waiting.

The writer of the book of Hebrews wrote these beautiful words: *"Let us run with endurance the race God has set before us. We do this by keeping our eyes on Jesus, the champion who initiates and perfects our faith"* (Hebrews 12:1b-2a, NLT).

We are in this race for the long haul. Because our children will likely not outgrow their mental or emotional disorders, we'll need great endurance to meet the various challenges we face and to finish this race well. Those who are navigating this race successfully are those who have learned to keep their eyes on Jesus, allowing the light of His presence to strengthen and sustain them.

When we allow the brightness of Jesus' face to shine over our circumstances, we will bring to light some surprising gems of God's grace—secret riches only God would have had the imagination to hide there.

My pastor once described God's grace as, "God's greatest surprise and God's constant disguise."[3] And it's true. Jesus seems to prefer working in surprising, unexpected ways. For many parents who find themselves in the pit of their child's mental illness, God's grace has shown up in some pretty amazing ways and has been cloaked in some very unique disguises. Following the flow of God's grace, these parents have learned how to turn their problems into possibilities.

Mike and Becky are living this out. Their son, Jeremy, was a handful from a very young age. Jeremy struggled with severe sensory issues, was extremely strong-willed and seemed to have no fear. He did not get along with other children, and school was a struggle from day one. Jeremy hated loud noises and large crowds. Sunday worship services, therefore, were especially trying. Jeremy couldn't tolerate the music in church, so his dad often took him out to a separate room.

Jeremy struggled with how to express himself in words and was very reactive to situations, often getting into fights. As a young boy, he had many "strange" behaviors, which set him apart from his peers. By age fourteen, Jeremy was diagnosed with Asperger syndrome. His growing-up years were very challenging. He often ran away, became involved with drugs and alcohol, dropped out of school, was placed in various residential facilities and eventually spent time in prison.

Now, well into adulthood, Jeremy continues to struggle with emotional health issues. He is unable to manage his finances, so Mike oversees his money and gives him a monthly stipend. He still struggles with relationships and how to relate to others. He finds it difficult to maintain a job and is often unemployed. Even though things are better than they used to be, Mike and Becky are concerned about his ongoing drug and alcohol use. "There's still a lot about Jeremy that we don't know. Though we're seeing some growth and progress in him, the reality of his life is very difficult."

Early in the game, Mike and Becky knew their relationship with God would need to see them through. Even during Jeremy's most tumultuous years, their faith remained strong and intact, though they often had more questions than answers. "Our faith never wavered; we never doubted. We kept the Word in front of us and continue to do so. That's the real thing! This life on earth is very temporal."

Today Mike and Becky continue to live out their strong faith in loving, practical ways. A few years ago they purchased a small house for Jeremy. They're very aware that from time-to-time Jeremy has homeless people living with him. Mike says, somewhat tongue-in-cheek, "Now we're running a homeless shelter!" Mike and Becky make sure there's food in Jeremy's house and that things are in working order. Even in this challenge, they see the hand of God. Mike stated, "Since Jeremy occasionally has homeless people crashing with him, these people are in *our* lives as well." Mike and Becky realize they can be an influence and encouragement to others who find themselves living in the margins of society.

Mike and Becky do not have a Pollyanna view of life. This is not the life they would have chosen, and they freely admit they often feel the weight and strain of their son's struggles. Yet they also testify that because of their difficulties with Jeremy, they've grown closer to the Lord and closer to each other. God has grown them in very tangible ways. They both recognize that God has given them a deep desire to help others. Becky realizes that she is much less judgmental and much more empathetic to those who struggle with mental health issues. Mike has been on several overseas mission trips and loves bringing the hope of Christ to those struggling in third-world countries.

Mike and Becky have learned how to rise above and live a sweet life, even in the continued muck of mental health challenges. They enjoy sharing the sweet fragrance of Christ wherever He places them.

"But thank God! He has made us his captives and continues to lead us along in Christ's triumphal procession. Now he uses us to spread the knowledge of Christ everywhere, like a sweet perfume. Our lives are a Christ-like fragrance rising up to God" (2 Cor. 2:14-15, NLT).

Additional Scripture to meditate on

*I will give you treasures hidden in the darkness — secret riches.
I will do this so you may know that I am the Lord, the God of
Israel, the one who calls you by name. (Isaiah 45:3, NLT)*

*So we're not giving up. How could we! Even though on the
outside it often looks like things are falling apart on us, on
the inside, where God is making new life, not a day goes by
without his unfolding grace. These hard times are small pota-
toes compared to the coming good times, the lavish celebration
prepared for us. There's far more here than meets the eye. The
things we see now are here today, gone tomorrow. But the things
we can't see now will last forever. (2 Cor. 4:16-18, MSG)*

*With every sun's rising, surprise us with Your love, satisfy us
with Your kindness. Then we will sing with joy and celebrate
every day we are alive. (Psalm 90:14, VOICE)*

A prayer to rise above

Eternal Lord, today we echo the voice of the Psalmist and ask that
with every sun's rising, You surprise us with Your love and satisfy
us with Your kindness. We acknowledge there are days and seasons
in which we find ourselves stuck in a pit of despair, surrounded by
the messiness of mental illness. On those dark days, Jesus, remind
us of Your promises and give us the desire to rise above our circumstances. When doubts loom large, may we choose to cling to You.
Thank You for the hope we have in You, knowing that regardless

of what this day brings, Your grace is sufficient and Your love is boundless. In Jesus' name we pray. Amen.

GOING DEEPER—GETTING PERSONAL

1. In the story at the beginning of the chapter, we read that Miss Agnes was able to thrive, not merely survive, following the deaths of her husband and son. What enabled her to rise above her circumstances and begin living in fullness again? Can you relate in any way to her story?

2. Do you ever find yourself struggling with "if only—then" thinking (i.e., *If only* God would do this or fix that, *then* life would be so much better)? Can you identify some ways God has chosen to change you instead of your changing your circumstances?

3. God's grace has been described as "God's greatest surprise and God's constant disguise." What are some surprising ways God's loving grace has enabled you to turn problems into possibilities, especially as it relates to the challenges you've faced with your child's issues?

CHAPTER TWELVE

Struck Down, But Not Destroyed: When Our Fears Become Reality

A GLIMPSE INSIDE

"Don't sweat the small stuff…and it's all small stuff." Right? Wrong! This saying might be a catchy title for a bestseller, but it's far from the truth. In fact, this sentiment is like salt in a wound when one's life has been turned upside down. I'll never forget the painful day we became *that* family. You know, the one on the local news—gossip-fodder for juicy news gatherers and Facebook commentators. Our son had been arrested on some pretty serious charges, and for us it was anything *but* "small stuff." It was one of our primary fears being realized.

When parents were asked what some of their greatest fears were concerning their child with mental illness, most had a ready answer. The number-one concern was, "Who will take care of my son/daughter when we're no longer able to care for him/her?" We all know the system is badly flawed—woefully incompetent to provide adequate care for those living in the grip of mental illness. In addition to that, many of our adult children have burned their bridges behind them and have a very small support system remaining. Their family members and friends are exhausted and burned out by their ongoing demands and challenges, and many adults who struggle with severe mental illness find themselves alone.

In addition to the concern of who will care for their children in future years, parents shared a number of other concerns. Fears regarding their children included:

- Trouble with the law, imprisonment
- Substance abuse, addictions
- Violence, abusive relationships
- Pregnancy, abortion
- Loneliness, isolation
- Broken relationships
- Discontinued education
- Joblessness, poverty
- Refusal to take medication, refusal to get mental health care or inadequate mental health care
- Homelessness, living on the streets, prostitution
- Their child's relationship with God, salvation concerns
- Suicide

Many parents expressed concerns for *themselves,* as well. One fear several parents mentioned was their fear of being falsely accused of abuse. Deanna shared, "Evan has an underdeveloped sense of danger and self-preservation. He doesn't always fear things he should and at times he gets hurt because of it. In addition to this, pain doesn't register with Evan as with more typical children. I will often notice deep bruises on him that I have no idea how he got. It's a very real fear of mine that people will think we're abusing him. In fact, one doctor threatened to call child services when Evan had a couple of broken ribs that we did not know about. We had no idea how or when he broke his ribs."

Michelle can relate. "When Lily is extremely upset, she self-harms. In addition to her mental illness, she has poor verbal skills, so I think this is how she tries to get her point across. Lily has had numerous black eyes (self-inflicted), and she once even knocked herself unconscious. Unfortunately, people do not understand. I have been turned in to Child Protective Services three times. To others, restraining looks violent and mean, but I restrain Lily to protect her from harming herself or others."

Still other parents related heartbreaking accounts of their own children angrily calling the police to falsely accuse them of abuse. These events were painful and embarrassing—extremely difficult for the parents to deal with. Even when the children recanted and admitted to lying, damage was done. Reputations were questioned, trust was lost and fears lingered.

Experts say that 80-90 percent of what we fear will never happen. It's true that our fears are based on unknown future events, and much of what we fear will not come to pass. However, the fears we have regarding our children come out of the known reality of our child's mental or emotional disorder. And what we know about mental illness statistics *is* sobering. The National Alliance on Mental Illness (NAMI) website lists several significant social statistics for those struggling with severe, chronic mental illness. Among those mentioned are high rates of homelessness, imprisonment, poor or non-existent mental health care, increased risk of chronic medical conditions, high dropout rates and high rates of suicide.[1]

Yes, our fears are real. And sometimes, for some parents, they become reality. Here are a few of their stories.

Lucinda's story—homelessness, pregnancy, abortion, abusive relationships

Lucinda reflected on the many difficulties encountered throughout her daughter, Haley's, life:

> As I look back on Haley's life it seems all my fears have pretty much been realized. Throughout Haley's life we went from one crisis to another.
>
> When Haley was young, I feared she would drop out of school, which she eventually did. I feared she would run away—and she did, several times. Then I feared she would become pregnant. She did, and worse yet, she aborted her baby without my knowledge. I feared Haley would abuse drugs and alcohol, and that has now become her reality.
>
> Right now, Haley is living in a very dysfunctional, abusive and violent relationship. She totally denies even having a mental illness and has quit taking her medications. I guess when I spell it all out, most of the things I worried about have taken place, except for one thing. I often feared Haley would end up in prison, but ironically, that seems to be the one fear that hasn't come to pass. However, now I find myself wishing—praying—that she *would* go to prison. At least then I would know she was relatively safe.

Yet through all this, God has been patiently teaching me to trust Him. I'm learning to relinquish things to Him that are totally out of my control, such as Haley's life.

Nancy's story—drug abuse, estrangement from family

Nancy shared with me the painful story of her daughter's drug abuse, pregnancy and ultimate estrangement from the family:

Mara, my middle daughter, was always a very, very difficult child. Things really spiraled downhill after high school. Mara was accepted into a four-year college, but she dropped out shortly before the end of her first semester. She had a difficult time keeping a job and became deeply immersed in the drug culture. Mara was involved in one tumultuous relationship after another and eventually became pregnant. Shortly after her daughter, Madison's, birth, the state removed her from Mara's care due to severe neglect. Thankfully, I was able to step in and legally adopt Madison when she was six months old. Mara now blames me for "taking" her child and has broken off all contact with me and her siblings.

The last I heard was that she is living on the streets in a large, nearby city. I'm at a loss for what to do for Mara. She refuses help, and quite honestly, our relationship is so toxic it's probably better that we don't have any contact. It all makes me very sad, though.

Dave and Joan Becker's story—life in prison

In her book, *Sentenced to Life²*, Joan Becker shares the story of her family's heartbreak and confusion in the face of a broken mental health care system.

Mark—the twenty-four-year old son of Joan and her husband, Dave—had struggled with mental illness for several years. In his early twenties, he was diagnosed with paranoid schizophrenia. Unfortunately, adequate mental health care was hard to come by, and the system inexorably failed.

On June 24, 2009, in a small town in Iowa, Mark walked into their local high school's weight room and fatally shot his former football coach.

When Joan received the devastating call that her son was involved in the shooting of Coach Thomas, she knew their lives were forever altered. In her book Joan recounted that life-shattering phone call: "I dropped the phone and my body began to tremble and shake uncontrollably. I remember my head falling to my desk. I started moaning and saying, 'No, it can't be possible. We have tried so hard to get Mark help…this can't be happening.'"³

In a later press release, Dave and Joan Becker wrote:

The last weeks, months, and years have been extremely difficult for our family to bear. We have watched our son Mark go from being a handsome, fun-loving young man…to a frightened lonely person trying to fight off demons too numerous for any of us to understand.

Ed Thomas was a victim of a victim. Although Mark and we, his parents, attempted to go through all the

right channels to get Mark the mental health treatment
he so desperately needed, the system failed miserably![4]

Only one life may have been taken the day Mark Becker killed
his coach, but an incalculable number of lives were devastated. A
wife lost her husband, two sons lost their father and countless others
lost a man they greatly loved and deeply admired. The Beckers lost
much as well. Their son and brother was charged with—and later
convicted of—first-degree murder and sentenced to life in prison
without the possibility of parole.

Though Joan and Dave Becker were plunged into a nightmare
few of us could imagine, they continued to testify to God's presence
with them. In their press release they affirmed, "God is with us;
God will give us strength to move forward and heal; and we will
continue to give God the glory."[5]

Lauren and Adrian's story—suicide

Lauren vulnerably disclosed her heartrending story of her son, Justin:

> If you had asked me to describe our son, Justin, when
> he was in elementary and high school, I would have
> told you he was brilliant! He truly was exceptionally
> smart—a genius. At times he was absent-minded,
> but generally he was happy, sociable, very intelligent
> and well-liked by everyone. After he went to college,
> though, things completely changed. Justin became
> more distracted than usual; his grades, once off the
> charts, began to plummet and were very bad. He
> became less social, preferring to be alone. His hygiene

became poor; he seldom showered or brushed his teeth. He also began to use drugs. Eventually, Justin dropped out of college and came home.

At first, Adrian and I thought the transition to college was at the root of all of Justin's problems. Several well-meaning friends and family members thought it was rebellion. But I intuitively knew it went much deeper than that. Eventually I took Justin to a psychologist for an evaluation. Justin was surprisingly open with the doctor, and when asked, "Do you hear voices?," Justin told him he did. When pressed further, my son told the psychologist the voices talked to him.

The psychologist suggested hospitalization, and my husband and I concurred. Justin, though, thought he could control his symptoms on his own and was adamantly opposed to hospitalization. As time went on, however, Justin continued struggling and we realized it was imperative for him to receive the level of treatment only a psychiatric hospital could provide. Eventually we had our son involuntarily committed. It was a very traumatic time, and I struggled with nagging guilt even though I knew it was completely necessary. In the hospital, Justin was diagnosed with schizophrenia and was placed on an antipsychotic.

Justin agreed to take his meds and attend therapy sessions. Even after achieving stability, though, he would still hear the voices speaking to him. I occasionally would overhear his "conversations" with them. In time, he acknowledged the voices were getting quieter, but they were still there. He also continued to use drugs, convinced they were helping him with his schizophrenia.

At the end, Justin was actually doing better. He was hopeful about the future and excited about going back to college. In fact, he was very positive about life.

I'm still not convinced Justin intended to commit suicide. There's a lot of mystery surrounding his death, and the details simply are not clear. Personally, I think he was just trying to reach another high. But regardless, our son is no longer with us. It has been the most difficult trial our family has ever had to deal with. We've struggled with immense guilt, wondering what we could have done—should have done. We all took part of the blame on ourselves. But God has been teaching me He is sovereign, even over this.

God's grace is getting us through each day. In fact, I find myself surprised by how the Lord has helped us. Just the realization that we've been able to go on with life shows us His great love and care.

Indeed, sometimes our deepest fears *are* realized. When fears become reality, what do we do? Where do we find hope? How do we find the strength to go on?

GAZING UP

"For God, who said, 'Let light shine out of darkness,' made his light shine in our hearts to give us the light of the knowledge of God's glory displayed in the face of Christ. But we have this treasure in jars of clay to show that this all-surpassing power is from God and not from us. We are hard pressed on every side, but not crushed; perplexed, but not in despair; persecuted, but not abandoned; struck down, but not destroyed" (2 Cor. 4:6-9, NIV).

Stories like the ones we just read are absolutely heartbreaking. Life in prison? Suicide? How do parents cope when their worst nightmares are played out in living color?

Lucinda told me, "I honestly believe we did all we could do for Haley. I know the worst thing we can do is to look back and think, *We should have…we could have…*After all, hindsight is 20/20. Now we just need to go forward."

Lucinda is right. When a crisis hits, we need to move forward. If we spend all our time and energy focusing on the *whys* and *if onlys*, our nightmare will loom even larger, clouding our vision and consuming our hope. We'll soon find ourselves churning in a whirlpool of despair. When our worst fears become reality, instead of focusing on our fears we need to intentionally move toward Jesus. He is our only hope. Scripture puts it this way: *"So we don't look at the troubles we can see now; rather, we fix our gaze on things that cannot be seen. For the things we see now will soon be gone, but the things we cannot see will last forever"* (2 Cor. 4:18, NLT).

How do we do this? How do we intentionally move towards Jesus? What does it look like to *"run with perseverance…fixing our eyes on Jesus,"* as we're told in Heb. 12:2? Christian author and speaker Graham Cooke suggests, "When faced with a new trial or difficult situation, ask yourself these two questions: *Has God changed? Is anything too hard for God?* This is a great starting place when a new trial comes into your life. Then search Scripture to discover what promises of God apply to your situation."[6]

If you're unsure of the promises of God, don't despair. God has not hidden them from us; in fact, they're very easy to find! Check out a good website or Bible app[7] and start searching. What specific promises of God are you desperate for during this difficult season? Are you longing for *hope* or *peace?* Is your *trust* in God depleted? Are you wondering why God is making you *wait?* Are you looking for *direction* or *guidance?* Are you feeling *weak*, yearning for *strength* and *endurance?* Are you feeling *fearful* or *afraid?* Do you doubt God's *love* for you or your child? Simply type the word or phrase you're looking for in the search box and you'll soon discover promise after promise—Living Water for your soul. I've included a few of my favorite promises in the section **Additional Scripture to meditate on.**

As we move toward Jesus and feast on the promises of God, new hope is born. We find we can breathe again. When we intentionally hand our nightmare over to God, the scariness of the nightmare begins to diminish. A seed of faith sprouts, trust grows and we begin to truly see that God is in control and that He is perfectly able to redeem any situation.

On the dedication page of her book, Joan Becker wrote, "God is my Rock and my Salvation, and it is only through his grace and mercy that I can survive this life's journey. *'For from him and through him and for him are all things. To him be the glory forever! Amen.'* —Rom. 11:36." [8]

When the Spirit of God lives in us, the peace of God finds a resting place deep in our hearts. We may be hard-pressed on every side, but we are NOT crushed. Perhaps we have been struck down, but we are NOT destroyed! Today we may find ourselves flat on our faces, but with God's amazing power giving us strength, tomorrow we WILL stand again!

Additional Scripture to meditate on

When you find yourself in a difficult situation or a time of crisis, choose one or two short verses and turn them into breath prayers. When the waves of fear wash over you, simply begin to whisper the words of promise back to God. As Philippians 4:7 says, *"It's wonderful what happens when Christ displaces worry at the center of your life"* (MSG).

Here is some Living Water to refresh and strengthen you when you've been struck down:

FEAR

Be strong and courageous. Do not be afraid or terrified, for the Lord your God goes with you; he will never leave you nor forsake you. (Deut. 31:6, NIV)

Peace I (Jesus) leave with you; my peace I give you. I do not give to you as the world gives. Do not let your hearts be troubled and do not be afraid. (John 14:27, NIV)

TRUST

But I trust in you, Lord; I say, "You are my God!" My times are in your hands. (Ps. 31:14, 15a, NIV)

Trust in the Lord with all your heart and lean not on your own understanding; in all your ways submit to him, and he will make your paths straight. (Prov. 3:5-6, NIV)

HOPE

Put your hope in the Lord. Travel steadily along his path. (Ps. 37:34, NLT)

Yes, my soul, find rest in God; my hope comes from him.
(Ps. 62:5, NIV)

WAITING

Wait for the Lord; be strong and take heart and wait for the Lord.
(Ps. 27:14, NIV)

Be still in the presence of the Lord and wait patiently for him to act.
(Ps. 37:7, NLT)

ENDURANCE

Patient endurance is what you need now, so that you will continue to do God's will. Then you will receive all that he has promised. (Heb. 10:36, NLT)

When troubles of any kind come your way, consider it an opportunity for great joy. For you know that when your faith is tested, your endurance has a chance to grow. So let it grow, for when your endurance is fully developed, you will be perfect and complete, needing nothing. (James 1:2-4, NLT)

DIRECTION AND GUIDANCE

The Lord will work out his plans for my life—for your faithful love, O Lord, endures forever. (Ps. 138:8a, NLT)

I will lead the blind by ways they have not known, along unfamiliar paths I will guide them; I will turn the darkness into light before them and make the rough places smooth. These are the things I will do; I will not forsake them. (Is. 42:16, NIV)

LOVE

Who shall separate us from the love of Christ? For I am convinced that neither death nor life, neither angels nor demons, neither the present nor the future, nor any powers, neither height nor depth, nor anything else in all creation, will be able to separate us from the love of God that is in Christ Jesus our Lord. (Rom. 8:35a, 38-39, NIV)

See what great love the Father has lavished on us, that we should be called children of God! And that is what we are! (1 John 3:1, NIV)

To Answer Graham Cooke's Questions

HAS GOD CHANGED?

Jesus Christ is the same yesterday and today and forever. (Heb. 13:8, NIV)

IS ANYTHING TOO HARD FOR THE LORD?

This is an easy thing in the eyes of the Lord. (2 Kings 3:18, NIV)

I am the Lord, the God of all mankind. Is anything too hard for me? (Jer. 32:27, NIV)

A prayer for those who have been struck down

In Your name, Jesus, we invite the Shalom of Heaven to wash over us. Overtake the chaos of our fears and bring us to the resting place of Your peace. As we settle into Your arms, we hear Your quiet whisper, *"Peace I leave with you; My peace I give you. Do not let your hearts be troubled and do not be afraid."* Thank You for Your promise to never leave or abandon us. We're trusting in You, Lord; our times are in Your hands. Amen.

GOING DEEPER—GETTING PERSONAL

1. What were or are some of your greatest fears concerning your child?

2. Have any of your deepest fears for your child been realized? If so, how did you find the strength to go on? How did you experience God's faithfulness even in the midst of your difficult new reality?

3. When waves of fear wash over you, how do you regain hope and peace?

CHAPTER THIRTEEN

Self-Care—Soul-Care: Securing Our Oxygen Masks

A GLIMPSE INSIDE

The struggle is real.

Barbara's daughter, Olivia, is a twenty-something who has battled severe emotional instability her entire life. Olivia saw her first psychiatrist at age six and has been seen by a number of psychiatrists and behavioral therapists since then. Throughout the years she received various diagnoses, including developmental disability, fetal alcohol syndrome and autism spectrum disorder. Barbara shared, "We knew by age three there was something different about Olivia. She was off-the-charts difficult. She created chaos all around her and was very aggressive. We often described her as the 'Tasmanian devil on steroids!' By age six, Olivia started showing signs of possible psychosis. By age twelve, she was hallucinating and acting out even more violently. After several hospitalizations and one arrest, Olivia was eventually diagnosed with schizoaffective disorder. Olivia endured several med trial and errors before eventually finding a drug combination that seemed to be effective." Barbara went on to say, "We're thankful that Olivia is more stable now than she has been in the past, and we're praying this will continue."

Living with a child like Olivia causes untold amounts of stress. A quick web search of the top ten causes of stress reveals that having a chronically ill child makes the cut for most every list; in fact, it's often listed as one of the top five major stressors. Not only that, many parents who have a child with chronic mental illness also fall into other high-level categories of stress. Financial difficulties are one of the top stressors many of our families deal with. Parents miss a lot of work bringing their children to various doctor and therapy appointments, as well as tending to crises in the home. An incalculable amount of money is spent each year on medications, counselors, doctors, hospitalizations, residential treatments, etc. These financial struggles are exasperated even more in single-parent homes or homes with only one wage earner. And unfortunately, the financial stress doesn't necessarily end when the child reaches adulthood. Interviews with parents who have adult children living with severe, chronic mental health disorders revealed that financial help is still frequently needed, even as their children approach their thirties and forties.

Relationship issues are another stressor typically found on the top-ten list. Parents of children living with severe mental and emotional health disorders report having relationship difficulties on most every level. They often struggle in their marriages, as both spouses deal with the ongoing turmoil in their home in different ways. Strained relationships with their other children, as we will explore in greater detail in Chapter 14, is also common. Siblings may feel resentful of the time and energy their parents devote to the squeaky wheel in their family. The other children are often embarrassed by their troubled sibling or even traumatized by their behaviors. Relationships outside the home are affected in negative ways as well. Parents of a child with a mental illness or emotional disorder often feel judged, misunderstood, ignored, invalidated and criticized by others. Because of this, relationships within their extended families, with friends, with church members or with co-workers are often affected in negative ways.

So yes, the struggle is real. Boil together a daily dose of chronic mental illness, financial difficulties and relationship issues, and you have the recipe for a stress-filled life of chaos.

Meagan's daughter, Amelia, has a long history of treatment-resistant chronic depression. In addition to her depression, Amelia also has a diagnosis of generalized anxiety disorder and agoraphobia and is believed to be on the high-functioning end of the autism spectrum. Amelia had her first major panic attack in middle school and needed to be taught at home for a while. For years Amelia's anxiety was so severe that Meagan and her husband could not leave her alone for any amount of time. They took turns attending church and going to extended family gatherings; they went alone to work-related functions, and they pretty much dropped off their friends' social radar.

Meagan readily admits that the stress and strain of navigating Amelia's chronic mental illness has taken an incredible toll on her *own* physical and emotional health. Meagan struggles with bouts of depression, as well as a list of physical difficulties such as fibromyalgia, diabetes and inflammatory arthritis.

Unfortunately, Meagan is not an anomaly. Many parents of children with severe emotional challenges painfully struggle with the effects of stress brought on by the never-ending chaos in their lives. However, when told by our doctors, pastors or counselors the importance of taking care of *ourselves*, we often feel somewhat resistant or even uncomfortable. Oftentimes we're just too tired dealing with *life* to add one more thing (i.e., exercise) to our day. Or we may feel selfish carving out time for ourselves, thinking it's taking us away from the things—and people—that are "really" important. Perhaps we've become what Joyce Meyer calls "pathologically selfless." Meyer writes, "We are to live sacrificially...but we must not ignore our own basic needs in the process. Everything in life must be balanced or something breaks down and quite often it is us."[1]

If you've spent any time on airplanes, you are familiar with the instructions flight attendants give as the plane prepares for take-off. One of the directives we hear is this: "Oxygen and air pressure are always being monitored. In the event of a decompression, an oxygen mask will automatically appear in front of you. If you are travelling with a child or someone who requires assistance, secure your mask on first, and then assist the other person..."

We listen with one ear as the flight attendants give their spiel, but their instructions could very well save our lives and the lives of those we love. They are intended to help us survive and function as well as possible in case of an actual emergency. If we are deprived of oxygen, we won't be able to help those depending on us for assistance.

This same principle holds true for parents whose children live with chronic, severe mental illness. The pressure and weight of emotionally and/or physically caring for such a child is massive. If you don't take care of yourself, you run a high risk of experiencing burnout, stress, health problems, depression, fatigue and anxiety.

According to the Mayo Clinic website, some of the more common effects of stress on our bodies, moods and behaviors are headache, muscle tension or pain, chest pain, fatigue, change in sex drive, stomach problems, sleep problems, anxiety, restlessness, lack of motivation, feeling overwhelmed, irritability or anger, sadness or depression, overeating or undereating, drug or alcohol abuse, tobacco use, social withdrawal and infrequent exercise.[2]

These are serious health risks—ones to avoid, if at all possible!

So, what does it look like to take care of oneself? This question was posed to the parents interviewed, and the variety of responses was wonderful! In addition to the foundational basics of self-care—healthy eating, regular exercise and adequate sleep—parents shared a wide array of creative activities they enjoy. God has wired us all uniquely, and He allows us to enjoy His gifts in fulfilling and satisfying ways—ways that bring life to our bodies, minds and souls. Here are several awesome approaches parents are taking to intentionally put on their "oxygen masks." Perhaps some of these will work for you, too.

- Participate in volunteer work.
- Get a massage once a month.
- Spend time in personal devotions and make an effort to memorize Scripture.
- Play with grandchildren.
- Take long walks alone.
- Listen to inspirational messages on the radio or online.
- Don't watch the news if you're struggling with your own fears and sadness.
- Go to the gym, swim, run, golf, play tennis, bike, kayak, participate in yoga, etc.
- Occasionally watch "mindless" TV, play computer games, surf YouTube or Pinterest.
- Enjoy going to work and leave the cares of home behind for a few hours every day.
- Retire early from work.

- Enjoy hobbies like gardening, knitting, reading, baking, etc.
- Continue to use the talents and skills you enjoy (i.e., playing or singing in a band, participating in community sports, etc.).
- Keep your schedule to a minimum, planning for some downtime in the week.
- Participate in Bible studies at church or online.
- Maintain friendships. Occasionally go for coffee or lunch with a trusted friend.
- Pull away from friends who are not positive.
- Yell encouragements to yourself, such as, "You're a SAINT! You do WONDERFUL things!"
- Take a break from reading books and articles on mental illness.
- Play Christian music at home, in the car, in the office.
- Exercise and eat healthy meals.
- Laugh!
- Stay home and enjoy an occasional quiet day. Do things that are fulfilling for you: watch TV, bake some goodies, take a nap, read a novel, etc.
- Go to a peaceful location (indoors or outdoors) and enjoy a personal retreat day. Bring along your Bible, journal or other reading material and spend a quiet day with the Lord.
- Enjoy nature.
- Sit out on your porch swing.
- Journal.
- Take lots of baths!
- Remind yourself to not look too far ahead. When feeling overwhelmed by circumstances, try to just do the next thing.

Aren't these great?! If you don't make a plan to intentionally take care of yourself, one day will bleed into the next, and the compounded stress will eventually erode your health. In time, your well-being—your spiritual, mental and physical health—*will* suffer.

Are you aware of how incredibly much your Heavenly Father treasures you and delights in you? He holds you in high regard! Perhaps you've forgotten how valuable you are—not only to your family, but also to your Creator. In fact, He identifies you as His very special work of art. *"You are God's masterpiece. He created you anew in Christ Jesus, so you can do the good things he planned for you long ago"* *(Eph. 2:10, NLT, personalized).*

Loving and caring for your difficult child may be the most important good thing (see above verse) you were created for. Just don't forget to love and take care of yourself, too! You are a beautiful masterpiece, fashioned and designed by the Creator of the Universe. He thinks you're worth it.

GAZING UP

"Have you forgotten that your body is the temple of the Holy Spirit, who lives in you, and that you are not the owner of your own body? You have been bought, and at what a price! Therefore bring glory to God in both your body and your spirit, for they both belong to him" (1 Cor. 6:19-20, PHILLIPS).

Indeed, our bodies are sacred vessels—temples of the Holy Spirit. Believers carry within them the very Presence of the Lord! Therefore, it is absolutely vital, right and necessary to take good care of our bodies. Jesus, however, knows that if we begin and end self-care by only tending to our *physical* needs, we will fall far short of what is fully needed to live an abundant, healthy life. One dad shared that he loves going to the gym and pushing himself hard, but it never entirely relieves his inner anxiety. He innately knows that exercise and self-discipline will never be quite enough to bring peace to his anxious heart.

Jesus absolutely understands the immense strain of being pushed and pulled in every direction. He, too, experienced the intense weight of stress and knows firsthand the bone-deep weariness it brings to the body. But Jesus also knows the weariness stress brings to the *soul*. And *soul-care* was always Jesus' primary concern. We read time and again of Jesus nurturing the relationship dearest to His heart by slipping away to a quiet place for some alone time with His Heavenly Father.

Jesus invites us to learn from Him. He genuinely understands the enormous stress our child's mental illness places on us, and He issues us a beautiful invitation to live freely and lightly.

"Are you tired? Worn out? Burned out on religion? Come to me. Get away with me and you'll recover your life. I'll show you how to take a real rest. Walk with me and work with me—watch how I do it. Learn the unforced rhythms of grace. I won't lay anything heavy or ill-fitting on you. Keep company with me and you'll learn to live freely and lightly" (Matt. 11:28-31, MSG).

When we are bone-weary and burned out (not just on religion, but on *life*), when our stomach is tied up in knots and our blood pressure is on the rise, Jesus quietly welcomes us to "sit down on the inside."[3] Jesus encourages us to make *soul-care* as much a priority in life as eating, sleeping, exercising and all the other wonderful things we do to take care of our bodies. He paints a picture of us walking side-by-side with Him every day. As we "keep company" with Jesus—walk with Him, work with Him and watch Him closely—we will gradually learn how to live unencumbered, regardless of our circumstances. And in those times when life is especially burdensome, He patiently whispers the much-needed antidote: *"Get away with me and you'll recover your life. I'll show you how to take a real rest."*

It's as if He unfurls a soft hammock in a peaceful grove of shade trees, puts an ice-cold lemonade in our hands and beckons us to *relax!*

These beautiful, poetic words sound so enticing, so appealing. But what does this look like played out on the field of life? How can we possibly live "freely and lightly" when our child is in the throes of chronic mental illness?

"When Andrew was in his early twenties," recalls Margot, "he began spiraling down. He had a diagnosis of bipolar disorder and had been on mood stabilizers and antipsychotics since his early teens. Unfortunately, he began to experience some adverse side effects to his long-term medications, which necessitated a med change. Things soon went from bad to worse, and Andrew became psychotic. He lived in a constant state of anger. He talked frequently about suicide and also began to threaten us. Finally, he told us the voices in his head were getting louder and louder, making some pretty scary demands of him. After one very tumultuous episode, we were able to have him hospitalized for several days. The psychiatrist who evaluated and cared for Andrew in the hospital diagnosed him with schizophrenia. He is now on different medication to help quiet the voices and reduce the hallucinations. Thankfully, he has achieved a tolerable level of stability. He continues to experience some symptoms, but for the most part they are manageable, as long as he stays on his meds."

Margot shared the pain she and her husband experienced during this turbulent time. "We felt so helpless watching our son spiral deeper and deeper into mental illness. We thought life had been rocky before, but this brought us to a whole new depth of pain. We never imagined it would be this way."

Margot knew she had some choices and decisions to make for herself as well. "My faith, though strong, was being tested like never before. I decided to make it a priority to continuously hand over to God my fears and worries and to go to Him for comfort and strength. I've had times in my life when I chose to turn to food or alcohol for comfort; but from experience I know their 'comforts' always leave me more depressed than before—filled with guilt and remorse instead of hope and peace. There truly is no substitute for the arms of my loving Heavenly Father."

The key to living freely and lightly—even in times of chaos—is to be in such close relationship with Jesus that we implicitly trust Him, no matter what. The closer we lean into Him, the greater our peace will be. This leaning in is a lifelong learning process, but Jesus is a very patient teacher! Here are a few ways to practice *soul-care*—holy habits that will help us live and walk in His unforced rhythms of grace.

1. *Stay connected to Christ through Scripture and prayer.*
   Spend time alone with God, reading and meditating on the timeless promises in His Word. When we tuck His ancient truths deep into the recesses of our heart, the Holy Spirit will bring them to mind in times of fear, panic, worry and chaos.[4] Speak to God as a friend and listen for His quiet whispers back to you. God speaks to us in countless ways—through Scripture, in creation, through the words of others, through thoughts and impressions, as well as from His Spirit to ours.

2. *Keep an eternal perspective.*
   We are part of a much larger story, and what we're going through is not all about us, even though it usually feels like it is. There's more going on than meets the eye. Our trials and our stories will interact with hundreds of others, and God has a plan and a purpose for each and every one. God reassures His children that though times of suffering are painful, they are nothing

compared to the eternal glory that lies ahead! Keep in mind that this is not our permanent home. Life on earth is very short, very temporary—just the introduction to the Great Story.[5] Though we can enjoy a fulfilling and abundant life here on earth, the best really is yet to come!

3. *Simply live one day at a time—one moment at a time.*

That's all God gives us anyway. When a crisis hits or a specific issue looms large and you feel yourself spinning with worry and panic, stop! Take a deep breath and remind yourself, God is I AM. He is here NOW, offering exactly what you need for this moment. Make a conscious effort to live in the present and not take on tomorrow's anticipated worries. Just do today!

4. *Release people and situations to God.*

Make it a daily habit to relinquish and release the people you love into the Hands of One who loves them even more. Release difficult situations you have no control over to the One who ultimately has the power to change things. Sometimes it's helpful to make a list of all the things that are currently causing you pain, anxiety, sadness, fear and worry. In prayer, very intentionally release them to the Lord and give them to Him to deal with. A prayer box[6] is a good tool for this exercise.

Jesus longs for us to come to Him when we're weighed down by the complexities of life, staggering under massive burdens. His life on earth demonstrated for us the key to deep peace and inner serenity—*soul-care.* Jesus modeled how to live freely and lightly, even in the midst of unfathomable stress, by making time spent with His Father a top priority. When we follow His lead and sit down on the inside, He offers our weary souls His breath of life. That's an oxygen mask worth breathing into!

Additional Scripture to meditate on

Don't you realize that your body is a temple of the Holy Spirit, who lives in you and was given to you by God? You do not belong to yourself, for God bought you with a high price. So you must honor God with your body. (1 Cor. 6:19-20, NLT)

I am the living bread that has come down from heaven to rescue those who eat it. Anyone who eats this bread will live forever. The bread that I will give breathes life… (John 6:51, VOICE)

Peace I leave with you; my peace I give you. I do not give to you as the world gives. Do not let your hearts be troubled and do not be afraid. (John 14:27, NIV)

Prayer for those living in immense stress

Lord Jesus, life is hard. There are times we can barely catch our breath. The stress we're often under is something we never imagined living with. Help us understand and recognize the importance of taking good care of the bodies You've given us. May we also be aware, Jesus, of the eternal importance of investing in soul-care. We accept Your invitation to come sit with You—to soak in Your presence and breathe in Your tranquility. Very intentionally we shift our heavy burdens from our shoulders to Yours. As we release our cares and worries to You, we sense Your peace permeating our souls and we can breathe again. Lord Jesus, teach us and give us the desire to live each day like this. Show us how to move and function within Your unforced rhythms of grace. Thank You for being our breath of life. Amen.

GOING DEEPER—GETTING PERSONAL ─────────

1. What is causing you the most stress in this season of life?

2. What do you do to take care of yourself physically? Emotionally? If you're currently not doing anything, what would you *like* to do? What are your interests?

3. Are you taking care of your *soul?* If so, in what ways? If not, what changes could you make to begin intentionally taking care of your spiritual health?

CHAPTER FOURTEEN

Siblings:
Ripples on a Pond

A GLIMPSE INSIDE

There may be no relationship…that's closer, finer, harder, sweeter, happier, sadder, more filled with joy or fraught with woe, than the relationship we have with our brothers and sisters.[1]

As you've noticed throughout this book, the focus has primarily been on *parents* who have children with a mental or emotional brain disorder. They are the ones who have been in the trenches—loving, guiding and protecting their children in the midst of countless storms and seemingly insurmountable challenges. But we would be remiss to not take a close look at the larger family unit, especially the *siblings*. As noted in Chapter 10, the effect of having an emotionally ill child in the family, like ripples on a pond, reverberates throughout the entire family structure. Siblings, in particular, are impacted in a profound way.

The questions posed to the parents interviewed included: "If you have other children, what is their relationship like with their sibling? Would you say their relationships have been affected in any way by their sibling's mental or emotional health challenges? If so, in what ways?" Though there were a variety of responses, 100 percent of them acknowledged that their other children's relationships *were* altered because of their sibling's mental health disorder.

Carolyn's response echoed the sentiment of several of the parents: "Wendy and her brothers don't really have much of a relationship. My one son and daughter-in-law send Wendy a Christmas card every year, but that's the extent of their contact. My other son has virtually no contact with her. But in their defense, Wendy cut herself off from the family years ago and makes absolutely no effort to rebuild bridges with anyone."

Linda told me, "Anne and her brother correspond only by email and online. They seldom do anything together, even though they live in nearby communities. Their relationship growing up was awful. There was always a lot of animosity and fighting, both verbally and physically. My son now has some empathy for Anne, but their relationship is still fairly strained."

Several parents mentioned their other children are often embarrassed by their sibling. Whitney acknowledged that her teenagers have frequently expressed frustration and embarrassment over eight-year-old Peyton's behavior. "It's to the point where they don't even want their friends to come over anymore. I see the resentment and anger building in them. Recently my older daughter vented, 'Peyton is ruining my life. I just want to have a *normal* family.'" Whitney said Peyton compounds the sibling rivalry by becoming mad and jealous when Whitney spends time with the older two. "It's hard to have quality one-on-one times with my teenagers, which is very frustrating."

When children become ill somewhat later in life, such as in their late teens or early twenties, the entire family feels the pain and confusion. Well-meaning friends and family members may acknowledge the emotions of the parents, but the bewilderment of the other children may be overlooked. Yet they, too, suffer deeply.

"Chase's two younger brothers were profoundly impacted when Chase had his first major mental health episode. The boys had always looked up to Chase, almost worshipped him, as their big brother. Chase had been a kind, gentle and caring brother—always very loving and sensitive. So it was extremely confusing and hurtful when, at age nineteen, his personality changed so dramatically. Suddenly he was angry, directing most of it at us. He became very judgmental, especially about morals, money, lifestyles, etc. He had grandiose thoughts and ideas and seemed to think he was superior and invincible. All in all, it was very scary—not only for us, his parents, but also for his younger brothers. Chase hurt both of them deeply by the things he said and did. He has since been diagnosed with bipolar disorder, is on medication and is doing much better. However, Chase's relationship with the younger boys is still some-what tenuous."

Sophie noticed the impact Alexander's onset of schizophrenia had on all his brothers and sisters. Alexander, a middle child, was a freshman in college when he experienced his first episode of psychosis. Even after being hospitalized and receiving a diagnosis of schizophrenia, his older siblings didn't believe it. They were quite certain he was just being rebellious and that he'd "get over it." The younger children, however, were very frightened of Alexander. Since they were still in the home when Alexander dropped out of college, they saw him at his worst and tried to avoid him.

Other parents, when asked about sibling relationships, responded with some *positive* feedback.

Judy said her daughter, Tessa, is six years older than Darren, who has an unspecified mood disorder. "Even though Tessa witnessed much of the behaviors Darren manifested in his early years, she was not, and is not, antagonistic toward him. She's a very understanding, empathetic sister and treats Darren kindly. Even though they have always led very separate lives, she wants her young children to know their Uncle Darren. I'm very proud of how she has accepted him in spite of all the trauma of the early years."

Deanna told me her middle child, four years older than Evan, is especially sensitive to Evan's needs. Evan, who is on the high-functioning side of autism spectrum disorder, can become very fixated on things and is prone to raging meltdowns. "Crystal is my 'mothering' one. She will bend over backwards to accommodate Evan and his wishes, sometimes to a fault. But she is getting better at not always doing that! She dearly loves her little brother and wants the best for him."

Siblings. Sometimes companions, sometimes adversaries—but always and forever connected by a familial link. Whether the link is a strong rope or a tenuous thread, whether it is acknowledged or largely ignored, we are bound by our family of origin. And it is precisely within our family structure that we first learn many important lessons in life. "Siblings are the people we practice on, the people who teach us about fairness and cooperation and kindness and caring—quite often the hard way."[2]

When one or more of the children in the family struggle with a mental health disorder, the lessons of fairness, cooperation, kindness and caring are indeed often learned the hard way. This was played out in our own home. Our son's mental illness had a profound effect on our two daughters. And the effects on them are as unique as their personalities. Even though our daughters grew up in the same household, their childhood views of life in our home are not identical. They watched life unfold through different eyes and from slightly different vantage points. There are so many factors that enter into this complex relationship of *family*: gender, birth order, personality traits and ongoing life experiences. It is impossible to fully untangle all the dynamics that take place within the family structure. Each life, each story is unique. Each person is affected in their own way.

So this part of the story is not mine to tell.

I knew this book would not be complete until a number of *siblings* were interviewed and allowed to tell *their* stories. While each one interviewed is now an adult, some of the siblings grew up with a brother or sister who exhibited mental health issues from a young age. Others had a more typical childhood, and their sibling did not become ill until somewhat later in life, such as in their late teens, early twenties or even later.

As with the parents interviewed, there was much variety in the siblings' stories. Yet one common thread ran through each narrative. Regardless of the diagnosis or time of onset, *having a brother or sister living in the grip of a severe mental health disorder was a life changer.* Those interviewed were impacted in profound ways, and their life stories have been changed by their ill sibling's disorder. Whether it has served to make them more compassionate and empathetic, or simply bitter and resentful, it *has* changed them. And each story continues to unfold as one season in life gives way to the next. Siblings, as well as parents, understand that chronic mental illness doesn't fade into the sunset with age.

So here are their stories. Here is a glimpse into a day in the life of siblings with a brother or sister* who struggles with a serious mental health disorder.

Carmen

Carmen's youngest sister, Monica, lives several states away, so by proximity they are not close to one another. But the miles separating them isn't the reason for the distance in their relationship. Yet through all the trauma and drama of life with Monica, Carmen is able to see the silver lining—a much closer relationship with God. Here's what she told me:

> Even from a very early age, we didn't get along. Monica was always quite different from the other siblings in our family. Even as a child, she was very difficult. She demanded to be the center of attention and always *was* the center of attention. In fact, to this day, she expects—and gets—a lot of attention from our mom.
>
> The growing-up years in our home were very chaotic. Monica was argumentative, manipulative and loud. She was verbally abusive to my mom and would constantly demand her attention. She yelled, screamed, argued and acted out constantly. In her eyes, everything was "unfair," and she definitely let us know that.

---

* As with the parent stories, names and minor details have been changed to protect identities.

Monica first attempted suicide when she was in the eighth grade. Because of this, she spent some time in a psychiatric hospital, but I don't think she received a diagnosis at that time. Since then she has been diagnosed with bipolar disorder. Monica denies being bipolar. She has seen *several* different therapists over the years, but if the therapist gets too close to the truth, Monica drops them and goes elsewhere. She seems to be in total denial of her mental illness.

Monica cycles in and out of our lives. I try to keep the lines of communication open by sending birthday and Christmas cards, invitations to family events, etc. Most of our correspondence is done by email, though, not by phone. The few times I've tried to talk with her on the phone just ended up making me frustrated and discouraged. Everything continues to be all about Monica. Without fail she manages to bring every conversation back to herself—*her* struggles, *her* needs, *her* life. She still operates from the belief that she is the innocent victim, and somehow twists everything to fit this model.

A concern I have is that she will someday publicly defame me or another family member on social media. It would not be out of character for her to post something very nasty, false or angry. She tends to get pretty unpleasant when she's down. Because of this, I'm very careful with what I post, since I never know how Monica would twist or interpret it.

One of my fears for Monica is that she would complete suicide someday. She is not in a healthy place, either physically or mentally. Even when she is doing fairly well, I brace myself for the fall. With Monica, what goes up always comes down. The silver lining, though, is that all of Monica's downs have brought me closer to God. I know He loves me with all my faults, and I know He loves Monica with all her faults.

I would dearly love to have a close sister relationship with Monica, but I know we can't and never will. I do pray for her all the time, though. I pray for people to come into her life who will be able to help her. I treasure the good times I've had with Monica and hold them in my heart. The happy memories I have with her are precious, since they are so few.

Holly

Holly's younger brother, Eric, has lived with a mental health disorder all his life. Holly has deep empathy and compassion for Eric, but she also admits her frustration with his constant and continuing demands for attention. She recognizes, though, that God has used her life experiences with Eric to help shape her into the person she is today. Here is Holly's story:

> I've always had a soft place in my heart for Eric. I just wish others had more empathy for people like my

brother. It makes me sad to see how people treat Eric and others who have mental health issues.

Eric is several years younger than I am, so we're not really very close. In addition to that, his life centers totally around *him*, so I'm not sure he's even capable of being close to anyone. He does call me from time to time, but the conversations usually revolve around his health. Since I'm a nurse, he'll occasionally call with a specific health question or to get my opinion about a disease he's positive he has. When I don't agree with him on his latest self-diagnosis, though, it usually makes him mad. He never just calls to ask about our lives or about our kids. Our conversations are always about *him*.

It was like that growing up as well. Eric always demanded and got a lot of attention. I would describe my childhood home as chaotic, noisy and uncontrolled. It seemed Eric was constantly raging about something. We never knew what would set him off or when the next blow-up would occur. I was frequently worried for my parents and their safety.

I'm glad Eric is living in a group home now. He definitely needs supervision to help him function and live in society. One of my fears for him is that he'll quit taking his meds. He did that once and the results were disastrous. I hope he'll continue to be closely supervised for the rest of his life.

Having a brother like Eric, though, has helped shape who I am. I know I am more empathetic, patient and caring, especially with others who struggle with disabilities. I work every day with people similar to Eric and feel I have a fairly good understanding of their issues. I believe everyone, including those who struggle with severe mental illness, deserve to be treated kindly and with respect.

Sheila

Sheila opened her heart and sadly shared with me the story of her beloved sister's drug and alcohol addiction, unrelenting depression and eventual suicide. She also quietly, but confidently, revealed the ultimate hope and comfort she received:

> My sister, Renee, and I were close to each other growing up. We were three years apart in age (I'm older), and we enjoyed being together. We grew up in a very strict, religious home, and Renee was quite rebellious in her teens and early twenties.
>
> As a young girl, Renee struggled with migraine head-aches and depression. At age eleven, she became addicted to a pain reliever. At that time (in the 1960s) they didn't monitor things so closely, and she took large amounts. Doctors believe she had some brain damage due to the overuse and misuse of this drug. Throughout her teens and twenties, she continued to struggle with drug and alcohol abuse.

When Renee was twenty, she suffered two major losses within one week. This affected her for the rest of her life. At that time, she was hospitalized with severe depression. Though she was hospitalized several times in her twenties, Renee never included us in her treatment program. From time to time she told us she was suicidal, but we never believed her. There were no signs, no evidence.

When Renee suffered one more significant loss in her late twenties, she decided she could no longer live in this world. She wrote a note to us explaining she had waited several years to take her life because she knew how deeply it would hurt her family. But now she felt she could put it off no longer.

I know Renee carefully thought out and planned her suicide. She completed it on her birthday.

This was by far the most horrible, devastating event I've ever gone through. Much of that time is a fog, but I clearly remember spending the first night with my parents. I vividly remember my dad wailing, sobbing out his regrets and pain.

There was a tremendous amount of guilt intertwined with our grief, especially for my parents. Forty years ago, though, we simply did not understand mental illness. It was not talked about. Plus, since we were not included in Renee's treatment plans, there was so much we weren't aware of.

My parents weren't the only ones struggling with immense guilt. I felt very guilty for not taking Renee seriously when she told me her suicidal ideations. I didn't really do anything to help her, and the guilt definitely added to the pain of my loss.

Following Renee's death, my mom desperately wanted to talk about her—*needed* to talk about her. She wanted to talk about the good times, the fun memories. But other people didn't want to talk about Renee—most were very uncomfortable with the suicide and with mental illness in general, so sadly, my mom did not get much support from her friends. In fact, one "friend" told my mom that suicide was a mortal sin and that Renee was likely in hell.

We know the truth, though. Renee had accepted Christ as her Savior and we KNOW she is safe in the arms of Jesus. And that was—and is—our greatest comfort.

Chelsea

Chelsea shared with me how her brother, Brandon's, mental illness affected the dynamics of the entire family. She conveyed her frustrations, irritations and fears of growing up with such a difficult brother. She is grateful for the supervision and help Brandon is now receiving, freeing her parents from much of the burden. Here is Chelsea's story:

My younger brother, Brandon, was always a pretty difficult kid. When I think back on my childhood, the first word that comes to mind is LOUD. He often had outbursts about things that didn't really matter. Anger was his usual mood, and he didn't care who he directed it toward. It especially bothered me when he took his anger out on our pets. He did not have empathy for anyone or anything—not for people, nor for animals.

It seemed like the rules my parents set for us didn't really apply to Brandon. He blatantly refused to follow them. When my parents punished him, he didn't care. The consequences never seemed to matter to him.

Growing up, I was frequently embarrassed by Brandon, especially when he acted out in public. Having a brother like Brandon totally changes the family dynamics. As he got older and his behaviors got worse, we had to quit doing a lot of stuff as a family. It got to the point where we couldn't even go on family vacations.

What bothered me most, though, was his lack of empathy and his aggression. I was especially afraid he would hurt my mom. As a young girl, it scared me when my mom had to call my dad to come home from work to help deal with Brandon. My greatest fear today is still for my parents. I'm fearful that someday he'll hurt them or kill them.

One of my biggest frustrations with Brandon is how self-centered he still is, even as an adult. That's one of the main reasons we don't have a relationship with each other. Everything is always about him. He never asks about my kids or my life, so it's hard to have meaningful conversations with him.

Brandon recently moved out of my parents' home. That's been good for them, and I'm happy that my parents finally can do some of the things they want to do!

Tammy

As a middle-aged adult, Tammy has unexpectedly found herself in the position of caregiver for her older brother, Rich. She is grateful to be able to share the responsibilities with her other siblings, especially the difficulties of navigating the mental health care system. Though Rich now lives in a nursing home, Tammy and her siblings continue to provide much of his support. Tammy beautifully articulated how she and her siblings care deeply for their older brother, as well as the grace they've received from their Heavenly Father:

My brother, Rich, was always very loving, sensitive and kind. Growing up together, there were no outright signs of mental illness. I suppose if we looked closely enough, we could probably pinpoint some telltale traits, but nothing too obvious. As Rich aged, however, his illness progressively worsened. After his first hospitalization, he was diagnosed with major depressive disorder, borderline bipolar disorder and OCD tendencies. Since then, he has continued to struggle greatly with his mental illness.

Rich's illness has affected his life in every conceivable way. Even though by nature he is very soft-spoken and gentle, when he is ill he can become verbally abusive and threatening. I think Rich's wife covered for him as long as she could, but she finally couldn't take any more. Rich has lost so much. He no longer has much of a marriage, is not able to enjoy a career and is not even capable of living on his own.

As it is now, my siblings and I are his main caregivers. My parents are quite elderly, but my mom asks about Rich all the time. She is very concerned about him and always wants to know how he is doing.

Our greatest frustration has been finding adequate mental health care for Rich. The system is so badly flawed. He seems to fall between the cracks, and no place seems to be the right fit for him. During the past couple of years, he's lived off and on in a variety of places. After Rich and his wife separated, he lived with my parents for a time. That eventually took too great a toll on my mom, though, as my dad is beginning to struggle with dementia. Rich then lived in an assisted living facility, until his psychosis worsened, and they said he needed to move out. He lived with one of my brothers for several weeks, as well as with me and my husband for a few months. He also tried living in his own apartment for a short time, but that did not work. Following a recent hospitalization, we were able to secure a place for him in a nursing home.

He's adjusted well there, and we pray he will continue to be able to live there.

Though it seems there's always one more hurdle to jump over, I am thankful that my siblings and I are able to work together to help provide the best care possible for Rich. We have cared deeply for him, in every sense of the word, and we see it truly does take a village. I could not imagine trying to navigate all this on my own. My siblings and I don't always see eye to eye on things, but for the most part we are united in our concern. Rich's illness has definitely brought us closer together as a family. We're still trying to fully grasp, though, what is ours to take on and what we need to let go of. Do we put our own lives on hold as we care for Rich? Some days it's not always so clear.

I'm thankful for how God has provided along the way, not just for Rich but for each one of us. I see, also, how God is changing my heart. I have a heightened compassion and understanding for those who struggle with mental illness. My prayer life, too, has grown deeper as I've been driven to my knees numerous time for Rich. I'm also immensely grateful for the large support system I've been blessed with. My husband and adult children have been graciously understanding, as have been my friends and co-workers.

GAZING UP ————————————————————————————

"You do not realize now what I am doing, but later you will understand"
(John 13:7, NIV).

There is so much in life we don't understand. We are not able to see the end from the beginning, and often we're not even sure what's taking place in the middle! As has been mentioned frequently throughout this book, however, God's ways are higher than our ways. And even though there are things we don't understand, we can confidently bank on the truth that God always has a plan. He knows what He's doing. And that includes the way our families were put together. God has a special place in His heart for family, and He carefully plans and fashions each one. Your family did not come together by a random act of the universe. The Creator of the world uniquely designed your clan.

If you have a brother or sister who struggles with a mental health disorder, it's likely that parts of your own journey have been frustrating and painful. As a mom of an adult child living with a mental illness, may I say I understand? I have seen the struggles my daughters experienced and have talked to countless others who have faced difficult challenges within their families. Many siblings struggle with feelings of being overlooked, ignored, pushed aside, misunderstood or underappreciated.

God sees and understands, too. He is not only aware of the difficulties parents have in balancing out the needs of their individual children; He also fully comprehends the struggles siblings have when one child seems to get the majority of attention. He sees and discerns how unfair this feels and the confusion it so often brings.

God's heart beats with love for you. He knows the frustrations you have had, perhaps for years. He knows the pain you carry in your heart. And He understands. He really does. He lived life surrounded by difficult people—people who wanted and demanded and took far more than they were able or willing to give. And yet He loved each and every person unconditionally.

I don't know what your role is in the life of your sibling. Perhaps, like Tammy, you have assumed the position of caregiver or even legal guardian for your adult brother or sister. Or perhaps you essentially have no relationship with your sibling. You live life cut off from your brother or sister—estranged and distant.

Most likely, though, your relationship falls somewhere in the middle. You love your sibling but recognize that your relationship will always look and function differently than what you would hold up as ideal.

No matter how close your relationship, though, or what role you have or will perhaps someday assume in the life of your sibling, God cares enough to help you fulfill it. And I believe the number-one role He asks us all to fulfill is that of love. Unconditional love. Regardless of how active or inactive you are in your sibling's life, God is asking you to show unconditional love. God knows how difficult this often is, yet He knows you are up to the challenge. And if you ask, He will be delighted to give you the grace and love you need for your sibling.

May this be your testimony: *"I thank Christ Jesus our Lord, who has given me strength to do his work. He considered me trustworthy and appointed me to serve him…Oh how generous and gracious our Lord was! He filled me with the faith and love that come from Christ Jesus"* (1 Tim. 1:12, 14, NLT).

Additional Scripture to meditate on

Live a life filled with love, following the example of Christ. He loved us and offered himself as a sacrifice for us, a pleasing aroma to God. (Eph. 5:2, NLT)

My loved ones, let us devote ourselves to loving one another. Love comes straight from God, and everyone who loves is born of God and truly knows God. (1 John 4:7, VOICE)

Three things will last forever—faith, hope and love—and the greatest of these is love. Let love be your highest goal! (1 Cor. 13:13 and 14:1a, NLT)

A prayer for siblings

Abba Father, how You love and value families. You created us to live in relationship, and the first one You blessed us with was our family of origin. You carefully chose for us the family into which we would grow to adulthood. Father, bless our family and our role within it. We pray for a deep love for our brothers, sisters and parents. Give us the grace to be able to love them with the strong love of Jesus. We pray for wisdom and discernment to understand and know our role as adult siblings. Bless us, too, with strong emotional and spiritual health. Where we have experienced feelings of rejection, resentment, jealousy or shame, bring release and healing. Give us the desire to choose forgiveness—for ourselves and others. So, Jesus, we invite You to come into the area of our greatest need and flood our hearts with Your love. In Your name, Amen.

GOING DEEPER—GETTING PERSONAL ——————

1. **For siblings:** If you have a sibling with a mental illness or emotional disorder, how has this affected your relationship?

    a. In your growing-up years:

    b. In adulthood:

2. **For parents:** If you have more than one child, how have their relationships been affected by their sibling's mental or emotional health challenges?

3. Do you agree with the statement that perhaps "the number-one role He (God) asks us all to fulfill, is that of love. Unconditional love?"

   a. If so, what does that look like for you?

   b. If not, how would you define your number-one role?

CHAPTER FIFTEEN

Final Thoughts:
Wish Lists and Moving Forward

A GLIMPSE INSIDE

I'll never forget the conversation I had with a mom several years ago. Her preteen son could no longer live in their home because of his violent aggression and unmanageable behaviors. He was a very broken child due to the severe trauma he experienced in his earliest years. This mom told me they were relieved to have regained peace and safety in their home, but it was bittersweet. Along with her feelings of relief and restfulness there was an aching sense of sadness and loss. Her grief was compounded by the deafening silence from others. She told me, "No one asks about our son. It has to be obvious to everyone that he's not living with us anymore, but all I hear from others is silence. No one at church asks where he is or how he is doing. No one in our neighborhood has asked about him. It's as if he were a phantom—invisible to the world around him. I think people are just so uncomfortable with mental illness. Maybe they think that if they just ignore it, it won't touch them or the people they love."

There is still such widespread stigma surrounding mental health disorders. It's a difficult topic for people to discuss, whether you're the one living with a mental health diagnosis or someone you love is struggling with one. Many negative attitudes and beliefs continue to be perpetuated about mental illness, bringing fear, distrust, stereotyping, ridicule and even discrimination to the surface. Too often those who are struggling sense the rejection of others. Because of this, many suffer in silence instead of seeking the help they need. This applies to parents as well. Those of us with children who have a mental health diagnosis all too often feel the stigma. We see the averted gazes and sense the awkward discomfort emanating from those around us. We don't want or need mental illness to be the topic of all our conversations, but too often it's an elephant in the room, avoided and ignored. So when we are asked about our loved one, it brings about a sense of hope that finally someone cares enough to ask! My husband and I appreciate it when a neighbor stops and asks about Kyle, when a co-worker wonders how things are going or when a fellow church member asks how they can be praying for us.

The final question to the parents interviewed was, "If you had a wish list of how others could help you, what would be on it?"

Reflecting on their answers, it was painfully obvious that the stigma of mental illness continues. And families are yearning for change. Parents long to break down the walls of isolation that seem to surround them; they deeply wish their children would be seen and appreciated for who they are. Parents want to be understood and believed by teachers, extended family member and health care professionals. They are profoundly weary of the misconceptions and the myths.

Many of the wishes the parents mentioned have already been covered in the book. But since these items seemed to be so close to the hearts of the parents interviewed, they deserve a closer look. In its own way, each item mentioned would help lift or remove the stigma that continues to stubbornly cling to the subject of mental illness.

If you are an extended family member, a teacher, a pastor, a mental health professional, a politician, a police officer, a co-worker or perhaps just simply a friend of the parents for whom this book was written, take special notice of this section. This is where you come in.

Our WISH List

1. *Respite care.*

   Without question, this was the number-one answer given. Parent after parent told of how difficult it is to get away, especially as a couple. Comments were made such as, "We need *time* together, even if it's just for a few hours. So often we have to tag team in order for one of us to stay with our child." And, "It would be so nice to have a place for my daughter to spend the weekend. My husband and I are never able to get away." Another mom wistfully said, "I wish I had someone who could hang out with my son for a couple of hours so I could go grocery shopping without him."

2. *Practical help.*

   One dad, who frequently travels for his job, said, "I know it would be such an encouragement for my wife if, from time to time, someone would offer to help lighten her load. She's often depleted by the demands of our son and would appreciate an occasional meal brought in, or even someone to run to the store for her." A single mom shared, "There are times I wish someone would offer to give my other kids rides to their school or church activities, since I can't leave my daughter alone. That would be so helpful."

3. *Befriend us.*

Many parents who have children with severe mental health issues shared their feelings of isolation and loneliness. "I often feel alone. I would love for someone to reach out and ask me to go for coffee or lunch. I don't need anything huge—just something to show they care." One dad said, "I wish people would ask how we are or how they could help us this week. Sometimes it feels like we're swimming upstream all alone." An older mom said, "I wish I had talked to others about the issues and challenges we were struggling with in our home when our son was younger. We lived in isolation—we didn't reach out to others, and no one reached out to us."

4. *Befriend our child.*

Many parents expressed their desire for others to reach out to their struggling child. "Our son is lonely and invisible. It would be nice for someone to befriend him. His social life, along with everything else, seems to fall on us. We dearly love our son and he loves us, but he needs and wants other people in his life to show him he's worth their time."

5. *Allow us to say "no."*

A few parents mentioned they feel a subtle pressure from their churches to be more involved in the ministries of the church or other Christian organizations. Yet these parents recognize that, for them and their families, they need to keep outside obligations to a minimum. One dad said, "My main 'ministry,' for now, is in my home. From time to time I'm asked to serve on the church council, teach a class or serve in a parachurch organization, but at this time in the life of our family I have to say 'no' to anything that would take me out of the home in the evenings. I'm not sure others always understand that." Along these lines, another mom shared, "I wish others in our church could understand why we seldom volunteer at church in any capacity and why we never volunteer in the weeknight ministry. Sometimes sending our kids to church on Wednesday evenings is the only break we get all week. We know it's a safe place for our kids to go and that they'll be with people we trust. Some people may think we're not doing our part at church, but we really need that break."

6. *Believe us!*

This point is especially geared for grandparents, aunt and uncles, older siblings and friends of those who "do life" with parents who have children with mental health disorders. "Please listen to us when it comes to our child's care—especially if our child is still quite young. We live each day on the frontlines, and we really do know our child better than anyone else. We know when they need to be removed from situations (i.e., at family gatherings), what foods or drinks must NOT be given to them (we usually have a very good reason!), why their schedules must be maintained as best as possible, why certain behaviors are overlooked and other ones absolutely never allowed and so much more. To you it may seem like we're hyper-vigilant or too uptight or much too strict or just plain weird, but we've been in this game a while, and we really do know what works best for our child!"

7. *Fix the mental health care system.*

Parent after parent shared their frustrations of dealing with a broken and inadequate mental health care system. One mom lamented, "The mental health care system is *awful*—especially for kids. Many of the residential places we needed to bring our child were very scary, yet we had no other options. Some places were much more trustworthy, but we weren't always able to access those. Something needs to be done." Another mother with an adult son told me, "The system is simply not working. Psychiatric hospital beds are typically full, so the emergency room has no choice but to hold our son for hours and hours, then send him back home. We need more places for people in crisis to go."

8. *Better education.*

One parent asserted, "People need to be better educated on what mental illness is and what it looks like. At the top of the list would be police officers. They are frequently the first ones we call in an emergency. It's helpful and reassuring if they have a good understanding of mental illness and how to respond toward those in crisis." Another parent very specifically stated, "We need to do a better job of educating the public about suicide and what to watch for. We need to better inform and educate parents, teens, college students, teachers, clergy, church staff, professionals, etc., about suicide risk factors, signs of suicidal thinking and so forth. We need to break the silence."

So there you have it! There certainly are other points that could be made, but these were some of the major themes that rose to the surface when parents were asked what was on their wish list. If you have someone in your life who has a son or daughter living with a mental health disorder, maybe you could ask them what's on their wish list. It just might be something YOU could help with!

GAZING UP ─────────────────────────────────

Speaking of wish lists, when I was a little girl I wanted to be a missionary. I dreamt of going to far-off lands to tell people about Jesus. I especially loved reading stories about missionary teachers who made such a difference in the lives of those to whom they were sent.

My life played out quite differently.

It turns out I still live in the same small Midwestern town in which I was born. I'm surrounded by family—brothers, sisters, nieces and nephews, aunts, uncles and cousins—not only from my side, but also from Steve's. It's not unusual to bump into former classmates, some from as far back as preschool! And most everyone in my community looks like me, talks like me, and several even worship like me.

So, were my little-girl dreams nothing more than romanticized yearnings? Or were they the quiet whispers of God's voice, planting a deep desire and a calling on my life even then? If so, did I miss my calling?

I don't think so! God is incredibly creative. He shaped His plans for me into a unique design, one individualized specifically for me. And it looked nothing like I envisioned as a little girl. When I was ten, I didn't know that a missionary could look very different than the men and women who brought slideshows to our Sunday school classes or that one didn't necessarily have to travel to Africa (they were always called to Africa, right?!) to be a missionary.

As I began to more fully understand *calling*, I came to realize that, regardless of where one lives, God's purposes for our lives will be fulfilled if we are open to Him and align our lives according to His plans. God's plans have always been to use us right where we are, no matter where that is; His desire for us is that we would be willing to step outside our comfort zone when He beckons us into a new opportunity.

Perhaps He's inviting us—parents who have a son or daughter with a mental health disorder—to break through the silence and stigma of mental illness and be instruments of change.

More than that, perhaps He's calling us to be missionaries of HOPE—men and women who shine the light of God's love into the dark, fear-filled world of mental illness. Many parents living in turmoil and confusion have a critical need to know God has not looked the other way. He has not forgotten us or our children. His hope and peace are available to all who are desperate and weary.

Throughout the pages of this book, we've peeked into the windows of our homes and families and have seen the chaos. Many of the stories have been painfully honest. It's hard to sugarcoat mental illness and personality disorders. We've heard the pain, witnessed the disruption and felt the despair of parents and siblings. Perhaps some words pierced deeply or brought sadness to your heart. Please know that was never the intent of this journey. My deepest desire in writing this book was to pour healing words of HOPE over despairing hearts, to strengthen those who have lost their courage and to offer life-giving words of grace and encouragement to those who face daily battles—and who too often feel they've blown it.

The end desire for this book is to inspire you to now take the baton. As God redeems your pain and brings healing to your emotions, He will also bless you with opportunities to share your heart and life with others. As you connect with Jesus and open your heart to Him, He will give you the beautiful privilege of walking alongside hurting souls as they pass through similar valleys of darkness.

Wherever you are is where you are needed.

As you learn to walk in deeper levels of trust and dependency, consider sharing your path with those whose trust levels are becoming dangerously depleted.

As you gradually discover what it looks like to fully release your child to God, embrace opportunities to share this freedom with those who still fearfully clutch their child with control.

As you let go of the pride that has isolated you for far too long, dare to unashamedly reach out to those who are still hiding behind walls of isolation.

As you learn to live in greater contentment within your difficult circumstances, open your heart to those still living in discontent, despair and hopelessness.

As God changes and molds you into who He envisions you to be, willingly share your story of grace and hope to those who are in desperate need of some Good News!

As a Christ-follower, you are the living expression of God's love. Your calling is here—live it well.

The Lord bless you
  and keep you;
The Lord make his face shine on you
  and be gracious to you;
The Lord turn his face toward you
  and give you peace. (Num. 6:24-26, NIV)

Additional Scripture to meditate on

I am going to put a special blessing on you...so that you will become a blessing and example to others. (Gen. 12:2, VOICE).

I waited patiently for the Lord to help me,
  and he turned to me and heard my cry.
He lifted me out of the pit of despair,
  out of the mud and the mire.
He set my feet on solid ground
  and steadied me as I walked along.
He has given me a new song to sing,
  a hymn of praise to our God.
Many will see what he has done and be amazed.
  They will put their trust in the Lord. (Ps. 40:1-3, NLT)

We can make our plans, but the Lord determines our steps.
(Prov. 16:9, NLT)

But my life is worth nothing to me unless I use it for finishing
the work assigned me by the Lord Jesus—the work of telling
others the Good News about the wonderful grace of God.
(Acts 20:24, NLT)

A prayer of blessing

Father God, it's reassuring—and humbling—to realize that though we can make our plans, You ultimately determine our steps. We're grateful for where these plans and steps have led us, and we trust You will continue to work out Your purpose in our lives. You have blessed us in so many creative ways, and as we go forward now may we be a blessing and an example to others. We ask for a new song to sing—a song of praise and joy, so we will be the living expression of Your love. In the life-giving name of Jesus we pray. Amen.

GOING DEEPER—GETTING PERSONAL ————

1. What's on *your* wish list? If you had a wish list of how others could help you, what would be on it?

2. How has God shaped your dreams, personalities and life circumstances into a calling?

3. How can you share HOPE with those around you?

"Now may the God of peace...equip you with everything good for doing His will, and may He work in us what is pleasing to Him, through Jesus Christ, to whom be glory forever and ever. Amen!" (Heb. 13:20-21, NIV).

ACKNOWLEDGMENTS

First and foremost, all praise and thanks goes to my Heavenly Father. I'm so glad I said "yes" to Jesus all those years ago. I am grateful for His patience with me and His willingness to trust me with this calling. Long ago the Holy Spirit reminded me, *"The Spirit alone gives eternal life. Human effort accomplishes nothing"* (John 6:63). I know my efforts alone accomplish nothing of lasting value. The Spirit is the One bringing LIFE to all things. So thank You, Lord Jesus, for bringing *life* to my life and *life* to the simple words I write.

Steve: This book is as much your story as mine. I was simply the one to put the words on paper. I am so glad God chose you to be my lifelong partner! God did an amazing thing when He put us together way back in high school. I am thankful we get to walk this journey side by side, hand in hand. Thank you for being an incredible husband, father, grandpa and man of God.

Stephanie and Kirk, Katie, and Kyle: I love the way God put our family together. God's plans for each of you are daily coming to fruition, and it's been a joy watching you step into adulthood. Kirk, Steph and Katie, you are awesome parents and have produced some amazing children! You love your children well, and I am so very proud of you. Dad and I love spending time with Konner, Haley, Kaden, Nikolette and Nakota, and we pray for them without ceasing.

Kyle, you are just the young man God created you to be. I'm so proud of the hurdles you've jumped over and the positive way you are moving into your future.

My mom and dad: I want to give a special thank-you to my parents. My parents are both now thoroughly enjoying life with Jesus, and we miss them very much. Steve and I are eternally grateful for the love and help both of my parents gave our children. Kyle and his grandpa had a special bond and I know Kyle continues to miss him greatly. My mom unexpectedly went home to be with Jesus shortly before the publication of this book. I'm thankful she read the preprinted copy and that we were able to have some good conversations about it. My mom was not only one of my greatest cheerleaders, she was also a beautiful example what it looks like to be "Jesus with skin on."

My family: Between my family and Steve's, there are currently 110+ extended family members listed out on my family prayer card! That's just my brothers, sisters, brothers-in-law, sisters-in-law and nephews and nieces (including great-nephews and nieces). I am indeed rich in family. Many of you have expressed love and concern in various ways throughout the years, and we've appreciated your support. I love my village! My brothers and sisters deserve a special thank you—Gord and Chris, Laura (also enjoying life with Jesus), Larry, John and Barb, Marty and Carol, and Dave and Cindy. Each of you have blessed me in unique, life-giving ways. We've always had a special bond. Not many families enjoy what we've been blessed to experience.

Not only am I rich in family, but also rich in friends. Many of you have shared my path for years, others just recently. I deeply love, appreciate and value the close friendships God has brought to my life. As with my family, I can't begin to list each of you out by name. I do, however, want to make special mention of a few.

Our Sunday night small group: Bryan and Becky, Jason and Val, John and Sandy, Nuper and Judy, Ron and Kathy, and Lisa—Steve and I consider you *family*, and we love sharing life with you. We've all had our turns sitting in the "middle chair" and experiencing the comfort of being wrapped in prayer. Thank you for faithfully walking this journey with us.

My Kairos small group (Anne, Becky, Evelyn, Judy, Kathy, Sandy and Val); my MOST support group; my Safe Harbor prayer group; and my regular lunch partners Amy, Sue and Jill: I'm thankful to be able to share life's journey with all of you and many other dear friends. I love and appreciate the incredibly deep bonds that have been formed over the years. A huge and heartfelt thank-you for being there through thick and thin.

And finally, a deep and sincere thank you to all the parents who shared their stories with me to make this book what it is. Thank you for vulnerably trusting me with your pain, heartaches and hope. There is something profoundly healing in the *telling*, and I pray each one of you will continue to experience God's healing touch as your story interacts with others. Please know I continue to pray over you and the lives of your children. I've never met many of you and likely won't this side of Heaven. What fun we'll have in eternity, finding each other and sharing the completion of our earthly stories! A profound *thank-you* to all.

GLOSSARY*

Antidepressant: Medication used to treat depression and other mood and anxiety disorders.

Antipsychotic: Medication used to treat psychosis.

Antisocial personality disorder (ASPD): See *personality disorders*.

Anxiety disorders: Anxiety is a normal reaction to stress and can be beneficial in some situations. It can alert us to dangers and help us prepare and pay attention. *Anxiety disorders* differ from normal feelings of nervousness or anxiousness and involve excessive fear or anxiety. *Anxiety* refers to anticipation of a future concern. *Fear* is an emotional response to an immediate threat and is more associated with a fight-or-flight reaction.

There are different types of anxiety disorders, including: generalized anxiety disorder, panic disorder, agoraphobia, social anxiety disorder and separation anxiety disorder.

Asperger syndrome: Asperger's used to be classified as a separate condition. But in 2013, *The Diagnostic and Statistical Manual of*

* Except where noted, these definitions are taken from two websites: The American Psychiatric Association (www.psychiatry.org) and the National Institute of Mental Health (www.nimh.nih.gov). Please check these websites for more in-depth definitions, treatment options, up-to-date information, etc.

Mental Disorders (DSM-5)[1] changed how it's classified. Today, Asperger syndrome is technically no longer a diagnosis on its own. It is now part of a broader category called *autism spectrum disorder* (ASD). However, many people still use the term Asperger's to describe what doctors call a "high-functioning" type of ASD.

Attention deficit disorder (ADHD or ADD): ADHD is one of the most common mental disorders affecting children. ADHD also affects many adults. Symptoms of ADHD include inattention (not being able to keep focus), hyperactivity (excess movement that is not fitting to the setting) and impulsivity (hasty acts that occur in the moment without thought).

Auditory hallucinations: Hearing something that is not real. Hearing voices is an example of auditory hallucinations.

Autism spectrum disorder (ASD): ASD is a complex developmental disorder that can cause problems with thinking, feeling, language and the ability to relate to others. It is a neurological disorder, which means it affects the functioning of the brain. The effects of autism and the severity of symptoms are different in each person.

The characteristics of ASD fall into three categories:
- Communication problems: including difficulty using or understanding language. Some children with autism focus their attention and conversation on a few topic areas, some frequently repeat phrases and some have very limited speech.
- Difficulty relating to people, things and events: including trouble making friends and interacting with people, difficulty reading facial expressions and not making eye contact.

- Repetitive body movements or behaviors: such as hand flapping or repeating sounds or phrases.

Bipolar disorder: A disorder that causes severe and unusually high and low shifts in mood, energy and activity levels, as well as unusual shifts in the ability to carry out day-to-day tasks. Bipolar disorder is also known as manic depression.

Borderline personality disorder (BPD): Borderline personality disorder is a mental illness marked by an ongoing pattern of varying moods, self-image and behavior. These symptoms often result in impulsive actions and problems in relationships. People with borderline personality disorder may experience intense episodes of anger, depression and anxiety that can last from a few hours to days. (See also *Personality Disorders.*)

Conduct disorder (CD): See *disruptive, impulse-control and conduct disorders.*

Delusions: Beliefs that have no basis in reality.

Depression or major depressive disorder (MDD): Lack of interest or pleasure in daily activities, sadness and feelings of worthlessness or excessive guilt that are severe enough to interfere with working, sleeping, studying, eating and enjoying life.

Disruptive, impulse-control and conduct disorders: A group of disorders that include oppositional defiant disorder (ODD), conduct disorder (CD), intermittent explosive disorder, kleptomania and pyromania. These disorders can cause people to behave angrily or aggressively toward people or property. People with these disorders may have difficulty controlling their emotions and behavior and may break rules or laws. The angry, aggressive or disruptive behaviors of people with conduct and disruptive disorders are more extreme than typical behaviors. The behaviors are frequent, long lasting, occur across different situations and cause significant problems.

Dissociative disorders: Dissociative disorders involve problems with memory, identity, emotion, perception, behavior and sense of self. Dissociative symptoms can potentially disrupt every area of mental functioning. Examples of dissociative symptoms include the experience of detachment, or feeling as if one is outside one's body, and loss of memory or amnesia. Dissociative disorders are frequently associated with previous experience of trauma.

There are three types of dissociative disorders: dissociative identity disorder, dissociative amnesia and depersonalization/derealization disorder.

Disruptive mood dysregulation disorder (DMDD): DMDD is a childhood condition of extreme irritability, anger and frequent, intense temper outbursts. DMDD symptoms go beyond a being a "moody" child—children with DMDD experience severe impairment that requires clinical attention.

Dual diagnosis: Having a mental health disorder and an alcohol or drug problem at the same time.

Fetal alcohol syndrome disorders (FASDs)[2]: Fetal alcohol syndrome is a condition in a child that results from alcohol exposure during the mother's pregnancy. FASD causes brain damage and growth problems. The problems caused by fetal alcohol syndrome vary from child to child, but defects caused by FASD are not reversible.

Hallucinations: Hearing, seeing, touching, smelling or tasting things that are not real.

Mania: An abnormally elevated or irritable mood. Mania is associated with bipolar disorder.

Mental illness or mental disorder: The term *mental illness* refers collectively to all diagnosable mental disorders—health conditions involving distress and/or problems functioning in social, work or family activities. These conditions involve changes in thinking, emotion or behavior (or a combination of these). Mental illness is common. In a given year:[3]

- Nearly one in five (19 percent) U.S. adults experience some form of mental illness
- One in 24 (4.1 percent) has a serious mental illness
- One in 12 (8.5 percent) has a substance use disorder

Mental illness is treatable. The vast majority of individuals with mental illness continue to function in their daily lives.

Mood disorders: Mental disorders primarily affecting a person's mood.

Nonverbal learning disorder[4]**:** Nonverbal learning disorder, or nonverbal learning disability, is a neurological condition marked by a collection of academic and social difficulties experienced by otherwise intelligent or even highly gifted children. The social skills that most people learn intuitively, through observation rather than by instruction, are lacking in children with nonverbal learning disorder. They are unable to perceive subtle environmental cues or learn by simply watching. Children with nonverbal learning disorder have trouble receiving and interpreting nonverbal forms of communication, such as body language, facial expressions, the concept of personal space or when "enough is enough" of certain types of behavior.

Obsessive compulsive disorder (OCD): An anxiety disorder in which people have recurring, unwanted thoughts, ideas or sensations (obsessions) that make them feel driven to do something repetitively (compulsions). The repetitive behaviors—such as hand washing, checking on things or cleaning—can significantly interfere with a person's daily activities and social interactions.

Oppositional defiant disorder (ODD): See *disruptive, impulse-control and conduct disorders.*

Personality disorders (PD): *Personality* is the way of thinking, feeling and behaving that makes a person different from other people. An individual's personality is influenced by experiences, environment (surroundings, life situations) and inherited characteristics. A *personality disorder* is a way of thinking, feeling and behaving that deviates from the expectations of the culture, causes distress or problems functioning and lasts over time.

There are 10 specific types of personality disorders, including paranoid personality disorder, antisocial personality disorder, borderline personality disorder and narcissistic personality disorder. Common to all personality disorders is a long-term pattern of behavior and inner experience that differs significantly from what is expected. The pattern of experience and behavior begins by late adolescence or early adulthood and causes distress or problems in functioning. Without treatment, the behavior and experience is inflexible and usually long-lasting. The pattern is seen in at least two of these areas:

- Way of thinking about oneself and others
- Way of responding emotionally
- Way of relating to other people
- Way of controlling one's behavior

Pervasive developmental disorder not otherwise specified (PDD-NOS)[5]: PDD-NOS was one of several previously separate subtypes of autism that were folded into the single diagnosis of *autism spectrum disorder* with the publication of the DSM-5 diagnostic manual in 2013. In the past, psychologists and psychiatrists often used the term "pervasive developmental disorders" and "autism spectrum disorders" interchangeably. As such, PDD-NOS became the diagnosis applied to children or adults who are on the autism spectrum but do not fully meet the criteria for another ASD.

Posttraumatic stress disorder (PTSD): PTSD is a psychiatric disorder that can occur in people who have experienced or witnessed a traumatic event, such as a natural disaster, a serious accident, a terrorist act, war/combat, rape or other violent personal assault. People with

PTSD continue to have intense, disturbing thoughts and feelings related to their experience that last long after the traumatic event has ended. They may relive the event through flashbacks or nightmares; they may feel sadness, fear or anger; and they may feel detached or estranged from other people. People with PTSD may avoid situations or people that remind them of the traumatic event, and they may have strong negative reactions to something as ordinary as a loud noise or an accidental touch.

Psychosis: Psychosis is used to describe conditions that affect the mind, where there has been some loss of contact with reality. When someone becomes ill in this way it is called a psychotic episode. During a period of psychosis, a person's thoughts and perceptions are disturbed, and the individual may have difficulty understanding what is real and what is not. Symptoms of psychosis include delusions (false beliefs) and hallucinations (seeing or hearing things that others do not see or hear). Other symptoms include incoherent or nonsense speech and behavior that is inappropriate for the situation. A person in a psychotic episode may also experience depression, anxiety, sleep problems, social withdrawal, lack of motivation and difficulty functioning overall.

Schizoaffective disorder: A mental condition that causes both a loss of contact with reality (psychosis) and mood problems (depression or mania).

Schizophrenia: A severe mental disorder that appears in late adolescence or early adulthood. People with schizophrenia may have hallucinations, delusions, loss of personality, confusion, agitation, social withdrawal, psychosis and/or extremely odd behavior.

Sensory processing disorder (SPD)[6]: SPD is a condition in which the brain has trouble receiving and responding to information that comes in through the senses. Sensory processing problems are usually identified in children, but they can affect adults as well. Some people with SPD are oversensitive to things in their environment. Others may be uncoordinated, bump into things, be unable to tell where their limbs are in space or be hard to engage in conversation or play. Sensory processing problems are commonly seen in developmental conditions like autism spectrum disorder. Note: SPD was formerly referred to as sensory integration dysfunction, but it is *not* currently recognized as a distinct medical diagnosis.

Traumatic brain injury (TBI)[7]: Traumatic brain injury is a form of acquired brain injury that occurs when a sudden trauma causes damage to the brain. TBI can result when the head suddenly and violently hits an object or when an object pierces the skull and enters brain tissue. Symptoms of a TBI can be mild, moderate or severe, depending on the extent of the damage to the brain.

ENDNOTES

Introduction

1. Dr. James Dobson, *Dare to Discipline*, (Bantam Doubleday Dell, 1982).
2. Ibid., *The Strong-Willed Child*, (Tyndale House, 1989).
3. Ibid., *Bringing Up Boys*, (Tyndale Momentum, 2001).
4. Ross W. Green, Ph.D., *The Explosive Child*, (Quill HarperCollins Publisher, 2001).
5. Dr. Demitri and Janice Papolos, *The Bipolar Child*, (Broadway Books, 2002).
6. Dr. Dwight L. Carlson, *Why Do Christians Shoot Their Wounded?*, (IVP Books, 1994).
7. Robert H. Albers, William H. Meller, Steven D. Thurber, editors, *Ministry With Persons With Mental Illness and Their Families*, (Fortress Press, 2012).
8. Amy Simpson, *Troubled Minds: Mental Illness and the Church's Mission*, (InterVarsity Press Books, 2013).
9. E. Fuller Torrey, *Surviving Schizophrenia: A Family Manual*, 6th edition, (HarperCollins Publishers, 2013).

Preface

1. Timothy Keller, *Walking With God Through Pain and Suffering*, (Dutton, Penguin Group, 2013), 264.

Chapter Two

EQUIPPED BY GOD: CHOSEN, TRUSTED, EMPOWERED

1. James Strong, *Strong's Exhaustive Concordance of the Bible*, (Zondervan, 2001), #2675 Katartizo, p 2029.
2. Philip Yancy, *Prayer...Does It Make Any Difference?*, (Zondervan, 2016), 58. Scripture reference used is found in John 5:19.

Chapter Three

FACE TO FACE WITH A "NO" FROM GOD: OUR DISAPPOINTMENT—HIS GRACE

1. The Gospels are the first four books of the New Testament. They contain the stories of Jesus' life and teachings.
2. See Matthew 6:33, 7:7-8; Luke 11:9-10, 12:31.
3. See James 4:2b.
4. See Isaiah 55:8-9.

Chapter Four

GRIEF: OUR LIFELONG ROLLER COASTER RIDE

1. Luke 2:25-35.
2. See John 11:17-44 for the account of Jesus, Mary, Martha and Lazarus. When Jesus' friend, Lazarus, died, we're told Jesus went to comfort Lazarus' sisters. He spoke gently to them and wept with them. His ultimate act of comfort was to raise Lazarus from the dead!

Chapter Five

THE COMPASSION OF JESUS: LIVING REfLECTIONS OF HIS HEART

1. Bev Roozeboom, *Unlocking The Treasure, A Bible Study for Moms Entrusted With Special-Needs Children*, (WestBow Press, 2011).

2. Mark 4:38 (italics added); read Mark 4:35-41 for the full account of Jesus' calming the storm.

3. Luke 10:40 (italics added); read Luke 10:38-42 for the full account of Jesus' visit to Martha's home.

4. John 11:21, 32 (italics added); read John 11:1-44 for the full account of Lazarus' death and resurrection.

5. Priscilla Shirer, *Gideon*, (LifeWay Press, 2013), 63.

6. Mother Teresa, www.verybestquotes.com/150-mother-teresa-quotes/.

7. You can read Joan Becker's amazing story of compassion and love in her book, *Sentenced to Life* (Credo House Publishers, 2015).

8. Read Jesus' challenge to Peter in John 21:15-19.

9. Teresa of Avila, quoted by Pete Greig in *Dirty Glory* (NavPress, 2016), 217.

10. Richard Foster, *Prayer: Finding the Heart's True Home*, (HarperCollins Publishers, 1992), 85.

Chapter Six
WILDflOWERS: TREASURES OF GREAT VALUE AND WORTH

1. Hannah Hurnard, *Hinds' Feet On High Places*, (Tyndale House Publishers, Inc., 1975), 42. This book is a beautiful allegory depicting the gentle, patient love of the Good Shepherd and the yearning of His children to explore new heights of love and victory.

2. Jer. 29:11:*"For I know the plans I have for you," declares the Lord, "plans to prosper you and not to harm you, plans to give you hope and a future."*

3. Rick Warren, *The Purpose Driven Life*, (Zondervan, 2002), 63.

4. See Psalm 139, especially verses 13-18, to catch of glimpse of our value in the eyes of our Creator.

5. Brennan Manning, *All Is Grace*, (David C. Cook, 2011), 192.

6. See Genesis 1:26-2:7.

7. John Eldredge, *Moving Mountains*, (Nelson Books, 2016), 46.

Chapter Seven

MAKING SENSE OF SUFFERING: OUR CHILDREN'S—OUR OWN

PART ONE

1. This prayer is based on a blessing written by Sylvia Gunter, *You Are Blessed in the Names of God*, (The Father's Business, 2008), #73, 133.

Chapter Eight

MAKING SENSE OF SUFFERING: OUR CHILDREN'S—OUR OWN

PART TWO

1. Stormy O'Martian, *Just Enough Light for the Step I'm On*, (Harvest House Publishers, 1999), 154.

2. These excerpts came from the Message version of Psalm 88.

3. Timothy Keller, *Walking with God through Pain and Suffering*, (Dutton, Penguin Group, 2013), 58.

4. From *The Hebrew-Greek Key Word Study Bible*, ESV; *AMG's Annotated Strong's Greek Dictionary of the New Testament*, (AMG Publishers, 2013), #2347.

5. Keller, *Walking with God through Pain and Suffering*, 191.

6. See James 5:7-11 to read about patience and perseverance in the face of suffering.

7. Bev Roozeboom, *Unlocking the Treasure, A Bible Study for Moms Entrusted With Special-Needs Children*, (West Bow Press, 2011), 64.

8. "For God so loved the world that he gave his one and only Son, that whoever believes in him shall not perish but have eternal life." (John 3:16, NIV).

9. L.B. Cowman, *Streams in the Desert*, (Zondervan, 1997 edition), 470.

10. Dictionary.com, *Redeem*.

11. Cowman, *Streams in the Desert*, 279.

Chapter Nine
CHURCH: DEALING WITH OUR "NO-CASSEROLE ILLNESSES"

1. Amy Simpson, *Troubled Minds: Mental Illness and The Church's Mission*, (InterVarsity Press, 2013), 110.
2. Ibid., p 37.
3. Mother Teresa, http://www.verybestquotes.com/150-mother-teresa- quotes/#sthash.GjKFmVU7.dpuf.
4. Robert H. Albers, William H. Mellers and Steven D. Thurber, editors, *Ministry With Persons With Mental Illness and Their Families*, (Fortress Press, 2012), 28.
5. Mother Teresa, http://www.verybestquotes.com/150-mother-teresa- quotes/#sthash.GjKFmVU7.dpuf.
6. Marjorie J. Thompson, *Soul Feast*, (Westminster John Knox Press, 1995, 2005, 2014), 40.

Chapter Ten
WHEN SATAN INTENDS EVIL: TREASURES UNEARTHED FROM DARKNESS

1. Oswald Chambers, *My Utmost for His Highest*, (original copyright Dodd, Mead & Company, Inc., 1935; Kindle version, Oswald Chambers Publications Association, 1992), May 8.
2. Dr. Adrian Rogers (1931-2005) was a Southern Baptist pastor, teacher and author.

Chapter Eleven
RISING ABOVE: FOCUSING ON JESUS IN THE MIDST OF THE MESSINESS

1. As told by Lisa Harper in Session One of *Hebrews: The Nearness of King Jesus*, (LifeWay Press, 2013).
2. "You Are My All in All," Dennis Jernigan, Shepherd's Heart Music, Inc., 1998.

3. Kevin Korver, "Recognizing our Brokenness" (see message archives, 08/28/16, available online at trcpella.com).

Chapter Twelve
STRUCK DOWN, BUT NOT DESTROYED:
WHEN OUR FEARS BECOME REALITY

1. www.nami.org/Learn-More/Mental-Health-By-the-Numbers.
2. Joan Becker, *Sentenced to Life*, (Credo House Publishers, 2015).
3. Ibid., p 97.
4. Ibid., p 130.
5. Ibid., p 130.
6. Heard on a Graham Cooke broadcast. See www.brilliantperspectives.com for more information about Graham Cooke.
7. There are a number of good websites and Bible apps. My personal favorites are www.biblegateway.com, www.biblestudytools.com and YouVersion (Bible app).
8. Joan Becker, *Sentenced to Life*.

Chapter Thirteen
SELF-CARE—SOUL-CARE: SECURING OUR OXYGEN MASKS

1. Taken from "Seven Reasons We Don't Take Care of Ourselves," joycemeyer.org.
2. This list was taken from the Mayo Clinic website, mayoclinic.org.
3. I heard Tommy Briggs (Gateway Church, Birmingham, AL) use this phrase in a teaching at a Journey to Wholeness in Christ conference (jtwic.org).
4. *"But when the Father sends the Advocate as my representative—that is, the Holy Spirit—he will teach you everything and will remind you of everything I have told you." (John 14:26, NLT)*.

5. This thought is taken from C.S. Lewis's quote on Narnia in *The Last Battle* (1956). "All their life in this world and all their adventures in Narnia had only been the cover and the title page: now at last they were beginning Chapter One of the Great Story which no one on earth has read; which goes on forever; in which every chapter is better than the one before."

6. Simply write out your prayer concerns on a scrap of paper, put it in a box and let them go! Give your worries to Jesus to deal with.

Chapter Fourteen
SIBLINGS: RIPPLES ON A POND

1. Jeffery Kluger, *Ted Radio Hour*, NPR.
2. Pamela Dugdale, thepeopleproject.com.

Glossary

1. *The Diagnostic and Statistical Manual of Mental Disorders*, Fifth Edition (DSM-5) is the 2013 update to the American Psychiatric Association's (APA) classification and diagnostic tool. In the United States the DSM serves as a universal authority for psychiatric diagnoses.
2. This definition was taken from www.mayoclinic.org.
3. These statistics were taken from www.psychiatry.org.
4. This definition was taken from www.psychologytoday.com.
5. This definition was taken from www.autismspeaks.org.
6. This definition was taken from www.webmd.com.
7. This definition was taken from www.ninds.nih.gov.